"Brainy" Neuroscience for Engaged People

A Handbook of NeuroChemical Leadership™

By Maria Paviour

"Brainy" Neuroscience for Engaged People

First Edition

Published by Isiliver Books

ISBN: 978-0-9543654-3-1

Maria Paviour asserts the moral right to be identified as the author of this work

http://www.mariapaviour.com
http://www.isynergizelife.com

Illustrated by: 'Jazz', other illustrations by Tate Paviour and Cole Paviour

The Numskulls ® © DC Thomson & Co. Ltd. 2015

Dedication

To service providers everywhere who do the most difficult job in the world (dealing with other human beings!) and still manage to go the extra mile; and to those leaders who are there to support and value them.

In particular, to those whose service has personally inspired me to tweet about them in my campaign to recognise brilliance at work.

To all drivers, especially, the "Super Bus Drivers" at Nottingham City Transport and to Karl Ward and his team of fabulous trainers, Dave Scarlett, Steve Clarke, Barry Hutton and Jacqui Poole.

1 The SuperTrainers at Nottingham City Transport

To Simon Kossoff and all the other CEOs who go back to basics to experience the work and listen to their people.

To my wonderful team of NeuroChemical Coaches™, Wellbeing Practitioners and Consultants who help me to make these ideas stick in the real world.

To Rain Hitchman and Jeremy Thorowgood for inspiration.

To the amazing business women of the Athena Network and to the Artemis Gang especially Lesley Roberts, Nicky Thomas, Emma Pearce, Fiona Hill, Cathy Strudwick, Mary Reed and Jeannie Gordon.

And last but not least, this is dedicated to Tracy Boylin and all those who had the courage to stand up and speak out about wrong-doing, regardless of their own personal security and despite horrendous bullying; the NHS whistle-blowers; and to *Patient's First* the organisation that supports them chaired by paediatric consultant Dr Kim Holt and surgeon Mr Edwin Jesudason.

Contents

Acknowledgements

Grateful thanks to the many people I have met upon my emotional journey to leadership.

Great big thanks to the inspiring Dr Helen Fisher for allowing me use of the Fisher Temperament Index and adding various bits to it to create a composite model of leadership brain systems.

Thanks to Mikey Stirling and Martin Lindsay at The Beano for permission to use the wonderful Numskulls picture.

In particular, my gratitude to the spectacular and inspiring leaders who helped to form the basis of this book: Elaine Aarons, Leatham Green, Mandy Brook, Lorissa Page, Dr Kim Holt, Petrina Mayson and Jill Finney . Also, thanks to Ben Andrews of KMG Health Partners Ltd for sage advice.

Thanks to the Awesomators of East Sussex County Council and to the managers - all of whom got fully involved with my leadership brain systems sessions– keep having fun and being "Awesome and Contemporary".

Thanks to Dave, Steve and Barry for permission to use their "Superdriver" picture.

Thank you to my PA Lisa Aitken for keeping me on the straight and narrow in every sense, to Polly Pomfrey for her usual creative genius, my IT guru Dale Harrison, Albert and Joan Clifford without whom this book would not have happened.

I must give thanks to my children, both in terms of the emotional support and for cooking supper and vacuuming while I'm still writing late at night; but also for their fabulous cartoons and drawings; Jasmin, Tate and Cole Paviour.

A special mention for the delightful Benis (and her equally delightful mother) for helping me with the final tweaks in cover design.

Thank you all for being extraordinary people and inspiring and supporting me on my journey.

Introduction

I'm not an academic. And so when I speak about neuroscience it's not with the gravitas of the many marvellous academics and inspiring authors who have paved the way to this book.

I am a business woman. And I've experienced good and bad leadership, as many of us have. But there was something about the good leadership that made my working life a joy; and something about the poor leadership that made my whole life a misery.

Yes, I had read all the manuals and research on leadership and management, and I loved the simplicity of the graphs and concepts – the question for me was: "why don't they always work?"

And the answer I came up with was that no model that deals with humans will work all of the time; we have a wonderful human habit of being unpredictable. So my mission became to look for what is most predictable about my fellow creatures, and my conclusion was this: the one thing we all want is to be happy, and the thing we do most is work.

And I knew intrinsically that when I was happy I performed at my best, and when I performed at my best I felt happy.

So, distilled down, this is really a book about happiness; about finding joy in our work, yes, but mainly, about finding joy in the relationships we have with our colleagues. When we ask our expectations to step back and we take in the glory of all the differences humans have to offer, we always will find new and wonderful ways to progress. That has been my experience. And as a result I've researched and developed a new kind of NeuroChemical Leadership™ – well actually, it's not that new, as I see fabulous leaders performing in ways I would call "neuro-chemical" all the time. Through studying these people who model excellence, and through working with amazing research and even more amazing researchers, I've identified what I hope will be useful ways of dealing with practical issues at work, and indeed, in life.

The reason I call this "Brainy" Neuroscience is simply because there is so much science out there, and I've selected the stuff that I think will be most useful and pertinent to leaders. For me, this is about being cognitively on the ball with what is happening, and at the same time, ensuring that you keep the thinking tuned in to the emotions. I call this being "affective".

My formula for NeuroChemical Leadership™ is

A+B=C

Or… Affective + Brainy Leadership = Co-creating.

Leading is about followers; and real success is about recognising that we are all in this together; multiple heads are better than one; but this needs good leadership to really work. It's not difficult - it's really easy. So I've attempted to make the neuroscience bit as accessible as possible:

Leadership is all about taking a journey to what is in your heart, and inspiring people to want to follow you there.

And a little tip - take a look at this smiling face every time you need an emotional, intellectual or physical boost:

Now let's get emotional…

PART 1

Emotional Leadership

"It depresses a manager to see his team cry…"[1]

Charlie Brown

---

[1] Charles Schulz 14th June 1958 http://www.gocomics.com/peanuts/1958/06/14/

CHAPTER 1

Emotional? Me?

Don't be ridiculous I'm a CEO!

"Don't expect me to talk about emotions...I'm an engineer...I don't do emotions at work!

Yes, someone did arrive on one of my courses providing that little gem of a caveat! My response was my usual response:

"When was the last time someone made you really angry at work?"

"Angry? Probably a few minutes ago!"

"And when did anger stop being an emotion? Hmm?"

I might add that I'm not usually that rude!! But I wanted to make a point here.

So to get off on the right foot I want to clarify that when I talk about emotions I'm not talking about 'welling up' over a picture of one of the team's new born baby – or more likely – cute puppy! (I'm sure more tears are shed over adorable little pups wearing hats and scarves and chasing their tails than anything else, but I could be wrong…) I'm talking about emotions as a natural and essential part of our human make-up and survival.

Actually, I'll go further – all our emotions are designed for survival.

And to get really clear about this I want to talk about the science of our emotions – so all you slightly tense people who have been told to read this book because you may need to stretch your Emotional Intelligence, hold on, don't throw the book into the corner of the room in a pique of rage …you will be safe here!

Emotional intelligence is not a fluffy thing. And as new research is being published all the time we are finding that psychology and biology are inextricably linked. We always thought they were, but now we are proving it. And as I studied both psychology and biology I'm feeling very much at home in this new world, and I am delighted that the theories I have been promoting for the last 20 years can now be recognised as not only based on excellent psychological models, but also on biological processes.

And what about survival? Well, emotions drive us towards those things that will reward us and help us to thrive, and away from things that will harm us and potentially end our lives. The way we see people's emotions in their faces is a vital way of reading whether they are likely to harm us or help us, whether they are someone to bond with and enhance our survival through safety in numbers, or whether there is trouble ahead. When we see the surprise or shock or disgust in their face that indicates that we should probably "watch out about that"!

Leading and Following

Before I begin talking in detail about leadership, the emotional revolution and the power of neuroscience I think we should begin with a basic assumption. Leaders need followers.

In the world of work we can be put into positions of leadership through unnatural means – that is, assessment centres and interviews etc. In the wild we may be beating each other with sticks, but thank goodness we are usually a little more sophisticated in our methods these days.

However, as wonderful as the selection process may be, and as well fitted as we may be for the role of leader, the process often tends to ignore the fact that the people we want to follow us may not want to follow us.

A conundrum we are expected to solve by being…Affective and Brainy; i.e. recognising and being emotionally responsive (affective), whilst keeping cognitively aware (brainy).

So here is the trick…being Affective and Brainy (A+B) is a daily, moment by moment thing. Being A+B is not a set of competencies; although there are competencies you can learn and develop. But it is not one set of these. It is being and growing into yourself; digging deep and applying compassion and humility. It's listening and learning; it's about being vulnerable and accepting this. Above all it's about remembering that as a leader you are nothing without your followers; that your role is not more important than anyone else's, it's just different and that if you do nothing else you need to learn to love your people and their happiness.

If you can do these things then you will attract and inspire people to follow you to the ends of the earth.

Being an effective A+B Leader requires you to develop your own way. There are skills you can learn, but the rest is up to you. The rest IS you.

In this book I can tell you how to notice what makes you Affective and how to connect and facilitate other people in being their Affective selves. I can tell you how to regulate what is Affective, how to find out more about what is not working and how to steer a path along what is most likely to work – i.e. being Brainy.

In the final analysis, I cannot give you a model that is guaranteed to work. But I can guarantee that if you apply these principles you will make big strides towards being an A+B Leader. So get ready to be you…only more so.

The Anxiety Epidemic – Especially in Top Leaders

As a psychologist I work with many top leaders, and I've noticed a pattern of increasing anxiety. This is also being fed back to me from my psychologist colleagues. Anxiety is becoming epidemic [2]

And not just in adults – I'm seeing many children who are also suffering from anxiety. And it is preventable.

My theory is that the working patterns of our lives now exclude the opportunity to have emotional responses within a safe environment. On top of this, we have extreme levels of stimulation from digital media and we have not just evolved to deal with this as we transition from one world to another.

For example, workload is as extreme as it has ever been. Particularly in public services where many of the employees are doing a job that involves handling human beings; social work, clinical care, housing, policing and many people are involved in customer service. For all these people the digital media should be removing the need for processes that do not require human judgment. My observation (from the outside) is that there is a veiled assumption that this will make the human part easier. Of course it will not. And furthermore, just because we have access to records and files does not mean that people can take on more cases without turning them into anxious people.

---

[2] Fineberg, N. A. et al. 'The Size, Burden And Cost Of Disorders Of The Brain In The UK'. Journal of Psychopharmacology 27.9 (2013): 761-770. Web. 7 Sept. 2015.

Expectations have risen in line with the speed of our computers.

But human interaction, although quickly processed in the brain is not something that can be quantified and measured in terms of time. We know that we all react at different rates and that we recover from our emotional reactions at different rates. And for many public service employees the most important part of their jobs is the part that involves dealing with the human being in the situation.

Of course, all work involves some human interaction and management. Even from people who carry out highly specialised work.

Numbing Down

From my experience of working with people dealing with anxiety there is a common theme, and that is the sense that all their emotions have been numbed, and so the only emotion that is able to be experienced is anxiety. Anxiety keeps knocking at our door until you listen and do something about it. And the more you say "Go away! Go away!" with your head under your pillow the more it will knock and bang and scream at you.

2: Numbed Badger, by Tate

In my work I usually help my clients solve the problem of their anxiety in six sessions. My clients start as "anxious wrecks" and leave as fully emotional people. Healthy and emotional. With just the right amount of anxiety – no, I don't send it away for ever for good reason.[3]

Why is it so many of us feel emotional = unhealthy? I argue that when we try to take this pathway that we claim is the way of logic and reason – in a Mr Spock from Star Trek kind of way – we are failing to be humans. Captain Kirk was a great icon of humanity – being always tested on and responding with his emotions which enabled him to make higher level decisions. And although Mr Spock could reason his way through dilemmas, the only real solution came from marrying this with emotion. Yes, I know that is fiction, but it's a great metaphor.

The word emotional has been taken to mean out of control of our emotions, but that is an unfair definition, as it prevents us for talking about emotions without making assumptions that they must be bad.

Our Subconscious Pester Power

---

[3] Rosen, R. (2008). *Just enough anxiety*. New York: Portfolio.

So how do we begin to tackle anxiety? First, we need to acknowledge it. Every time we feel it we need to tell ourselves that we notice it. Our subconscious will leave us alone when it has been heard. It's a bit like an annoying child. You know the kind, that employ "pester power" something like this:

"Mum…..Mum…..Mum…..Mum….look...Mum….look…
Mum….Mum….Mum…Look, look Mum. .Mum, look…
look, Mum,Mum,Mum, Mum..look..look..MUM!...MUM!
LOOK! LOOK!! MUM!! MUM!! MUM! LOOK! LOOK
MUM! LOOK MUM! LOOK MUM!!!!LOOOOOK!!!!
MUUUM!! LOOOOOK!!"

And so on and so forth. The subconscious never bores of this approach.

Acknowledge the anxiety knocking on your door – something like this:

"Oh hello there, Anxiety, so you're a-knocking, are you? Well ok. I guess I need to be aware of you. Thanks for dropping by, now off you go!"

And as soon as you acknowledge that the anxiety is there for a purpose it will diminish. It you deny or ignore it, it will never leave you alone.

Anxiety is just another emotional reaction that needs to be heard. It's your survival instinct kicking in. Don't fear it, learn to love it. Invite it in for tea and sit with it, just like you would an old friend who is really good at giving you tough love – the kind that say's "look, only your best friend would tell you this – but you have a bit of garlic breath" Anxiety is the same type of friend.

It will tell you what you need to hear, not what you want to hear. And if you are kind to it, you'll realise it's doing it for all the right reasons; in your own best interests.[4]

The Emotion Wheel

All emotions are important, negative as well as positive. Of course we don't want to dwell on negatives, but if we try to supress and ignore them we are heading for ill health.[5]

My work with my clients on an individual basis includes spending time reviewing the different possible emotions that they may feel in different circumstances. And for that purpose I provide the emotion wheel. This shows the core emotions and the combination of these emotions that create further

[4] Leader, Darian. 'Heed The New Age Of Anxiety Rather Than Bemoaning It'. Guardian 2013. Web. 7 Sept. 2015.

[5] Rodriguez, Tori. 'Negative Emotions Are Key To Wellbeing'. Scientific American Mind 24.2 (2013): 26-27. Web. 7 Sept. 2015.

emotions. By reviewing this and taking the time to ask oneself "what am I feeling right now?" we can begin to identify feelings other than just anxiety.

All leaders need to become good at this emotion wheel, because we are much better at recognising the emotions of others than we are of ourselves (although there are differences between us in this ability to recognise our emotions which I will explain). And it's also worth remembering that while you, as a leader may be feeling stressed, it is more stressful to be a follower – so it really does fall to you to support those people who are feeling stressed just because they need to follow you![6]

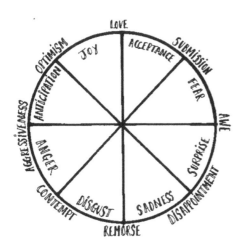

THE EMOTION WHEEL

3 The Emotion Wheel, after Plutchiks model (1980)

[6] Szalavitz, Maia. 'Why Being A Leader Is Less Stressful Than Following | TIME.Com'. TIME.com. N.p., 2012. Web. 7 Sept. 2015. Contrary to the common wisdom that people in

A tool for all leaders is a copy of the emotion wheel which can be used as part of a supportive conversation with followers.[7]

Susan Greenfield describes emotions as follows:

"In evolutionary terms we can view emotions as processes where one is highly interactive with the environment"[8]

So Dr Susan explains that when we are all about sensing what is going on around us we may not connect fully with our minds – with that amazing neocortex that is so very clever and resourceful. On the other hand, by pretending that we don't interact with the environment – pretending that the stressor is not really there, even when it is standing behind the door with a massive custard pie, then we are simply denying its presence and...whoops there's that old threat response banging at the door again!

We think we are making rational decisions. We think we are – but are we?

---

positions of power are more stressed than the rest of us, a new study finds that those in higher-ranking roles wield more control and, thus, suffer less stress and anxiety

[7] Plutchiks model (1980) in Zimbardo 1992

[8] Greenfield, S. (2002). *The private life of the brain*. London: Penguin.

As a senior manager or business leader we may feel a little embarrassed if we were to say that our decisions are made emotionally. Reflect for a minute, what reaction you might get from your contemporaries if you were to say that your decisions were made emotionally. Most people are stuck in the view that emotional decisions are as meaningful to business as the cute puppy in the hat and scarf.

If you think about it, a business is only as good as the quality of the decisions that it makes. So although decision algorithms can be helpful, they are not responsible for the quality of the decision – and in any event, if an algorithm can answer the issue, why not just write a computer programme and dispense with human beings altogether – and obviously, I do not approve of that idea!

4 School Monitor by Jazz

As far as our brains are concerned, decision-making is a behaviour that is governed by the limbic system; which is also the seat for the emotions. All our behaviours are affected from this part of the brain.

And this part of our brain is very old indeed – and shared with animals too. Animals have very intense emotions, and these are part of their, and our, survival mechanisms.

I read a fascinating and inspiring book called "Wesley the Owl" by Stacey O'Brien[9] and it certainly has helped me to review the way I think about emotions in general, and at work, specifically. Owls it appears are deeply emotional creatures. If they suffer a trauma or feel a sense of profound loss they can give up the will to live. This manifests itself in a very particular behaviour. For example, if a barn owl loses its mate it may perch in a tree, turn its face to the tree and wait until it dies. What a heart-breaking scenario. Author Stacey O'Brien talked about the importance of not laughing at the antics of Wesley her barn owl when he made comical attempts at flight, because they noticed that when they laughed he would turn to the wall, clearly emotionally wounded, even if he was not damaged by his crash landing.

Stacey O'Brien also recounts how snakes can be traumatised by a live mouse, if they are not warm enough to eat it. They're sense of vulnerability when trapped in an environment with an agile warm-blooded creature, whilst they are lethargic and

---

[9] O'Brien, S. (2008). *Wesley the owl*. New York: Free Press.

slow to react, can cause a fear that prevents them from ever attempting the nature process of consuming a live rodent.

All this is very interesting, but it is also very important. We need to understand our emotions in the context of social situations and our personal survival. Archaically our emotional responses were geared towards protection and ensuring the survival of the next generation.

Survival is clearly responsible for our ability to see danger and respond to it. But there are other ways we can protect ourselves, for example, the way in which we read each other's faces. Being able to read whether someone is angry or supportive is vital. When we smile at each other we demonstrate that we are friends and not foes, we do not need to fear or fight.

Romance and lawn mowers

When we make eye to eye contact with each other, we stimulate the bonding response, and we feel love (in whatever form that may take). In the world of work we talk about connection – because when we talk about love people get a bit nervous that it may imply a life time's commitment, marriage, children, school plays and lawn mowers; or worse, office romances and wicked affairs. So we run as far as we can from talking about Love at work, but a great many of us still manage to fall into the tender trap of romance and lawn mowers.

This fear of mentioning the "L" word in case it evokes an orgy of sexual madness is not.... how can say? It's not exactly healthy.

I've been banging on about this for years (yes, banging on – it's not a euphemism!!) So let's get over this dangerous four letter word and start accepting that the one thing we can't live without is love – (according to Will.I.Am[10] – and frankly, I'm there with him on this) and if we can't live without it how on earth do we think we can run a business without it. It's like saying "you don't need food to work". There's a slight issue here, in that although food is not directly required for work, seeing as we die without it I would say food is indirectly rather essential to performance at work!

By having emotions, and by displaying emotions, we equip ourselves and others for dealing with events that present themselves. Often these were more useful back in "days of yore" when our lives were at risk on a day-to-day basis.

---

[10] http://will.i.am/ singer songwriter

Now, it's our jobs that are at risk, or maybe our homes, or our reputation, or our status and so on. So the emotions that we feel – that were there for our survival – are now being applied to events that are not exactly life threatening. And often we would like to have a different way of reacting, but sometimes they just seem so embedded.

As homo sapiens, we have developed a higher functioning part of our brains, the neo-cortex (the new brain) and here we are able to construct language. The neo- cortex is where we are able to think rationally – and, therefore, we are able to rationalise. These two – rational thinking and rationalising – are different. When we are rational we are applying logic; when we are rationalising we are fitting reality into our model, we find ways of making what we are thinking appear rational.

Rationalising appears to be a process that happens very quickly. It has a big impact on our decision making and it functions a bit like the appraisal process in emotions – whereby we have an almost instantaneous cognitive response which feeds into the emotional response. Rationalisation, the attempt to explain or justify (behaviour or an attitude) with logical reasons, even if these are not appropriate, is an in built speedy process and we may not even notice it. [11]

I'll give you an example – have you ever really wanted to buy something that was not necessary and maybe expensive, and really there was no rational reason for buying it – but you remembered that you have saved money on your other shopping bill, and so, you tell yourself, really you have that (saved) money to spend on something else. Or perhaps you have not wanted to go to work, and so you reminded yourself that you are feeling a bit off colour, and it would be unfair to infect everyone else in the office, so it would probably be best if you stayed at home.

Yep! Rationalising.

So how does any of this relate to decision-making?

Well, when we make a decision we do so by tuning into our emotions. Of course, it is possible to make decisions based entirely on logic – but almost every time we will override

[11] The neural basis of rationalization: cognitive dissonance reduction during decision-making Johanna M. Jarcho Elliot T. Berkman and Matthew D. Lieberman [1]Department of Psychiatry & Biobehavioral Sciences, [2]Center for Neurobiology of Stress, University of California, Los Angeles, CA 90025, and [3]Department of Psychology, University of Oregon, Eugene, OR 97403, USA Received March 18, 2010. Accepted May 19, 2010.

logic because "it feels wrong" "it doesn't feel right". Feelings-huh?

This is not, in itself, a bad thing. Our emotions do guide our behaviours and therefore our decision-making. However, we need to be aware of this, and how we may be rationalising rather than applying pure logic. When you begin to review the decisions you are making you may notice this.

The thing is, if we are using our feelings in our decision-making at work, then do you think we should, maybe, learn more about the way negative emotions – our own "stuff" – can get in the way of making a good one? I think organisations may benefit from taking more time to consider the emotions behind decisions, and less time rationalising them.

And maybe, if we can lose the limiting decisions that we make because of emotional baggage we all carry around, we could find ourselves opening up our worlds to a whole heap of new possibilities and successes.

Just a thought.

Rationalising Decisions vs Rational Decisions

So let's start by reviewing the way in which we talk over our decisions.

What's the difference between a rationalised decision and a rational decision? I often in my workshops and events ask people if they have bought a house, and if so if that is the largest thing they have ever bought. It usually is.

Then I ask – did they have a list of boxes that the house had to tick. Yes they say... And did you buy the house that ticked all the boxes, or was it one that ticked most, or some. They look at me with a sideways wry smile, yes, they say, how did you know? So, I ask, was it an emotional or rational decision? Well, they say, it was mostly rational…but in the end they say that they chose the house that just "felt right" and few can say much more than that. It just felt right.

Then I explain that is because the part of our brain that makes decisions is situated in the limbic brain. This is the part of the brain that we share with animals. It's the part that is responsible for our emotions.

I remember one chap (who we shall call Gavin for no particular reason) disagreed that his decision was emotional. Gavin said that he bought his house for entirely rational reasons (by the way, Gavin was a lawyer – in case that's relevant). Gav (let's be informal here) said that he checked that every aspect of his house would ensure that he would be able to re-sell it and make the best return, but most importantly, he needed to be able to re-sell quickly if this was required.

A little later, after we had spoken more about how the part of the brain that is involved in behaviour is also the emotional bit Gav piped up; "Ah! I did make an emotional purchase! It was my fear of not being able to sell such a big asset that drove my decision!" For Gavin, this was a major epiphany. And I was delighted that I had managed to make my point!!

But seriously, we ignore our emotions at our peril.

Rationalised Decision
Based on emotions, but pretend that it is based upon some good reasons that we figure out after we have already made the decision.

Rational Decision
Based on all the factors, including recognition of our emotions.

In other words, either we go into denial, or pretend our emotions are not impacting on our decision making – or we acknowledge and accept their role, which will also allow us to make better analysis. Why? Because once we accept that we may have an emotional bias we can question and challenge that. It may not change our decision. And often won't. Because frequently our emotions are picking up on instinctive goals and needs.

On the other hand, sometimes, like with Gav, they are simply picking up on irrational fears. Maybe Gav's fear was well founded, but until he reviews it he will not be able to decide how well founded, or indeed, if he wants to allow that fear to make the final choice. It may depend on the level of risk he is prepared to take.

A+B REFLECTION

How do you make decisions?

Research proves that most CEOs evaluate the statistical data carefully but finally trust their instinct before making a decision.

For example, of sixty highly successful entrepreneurs connected with companies having revenues ranging from $2million to $400 million, just one said his business decisions were made using only the classic decision-tree methods– and even he added that his final decision was still made intuitively. The others all either used their feelings to confirm (or disconfirm) a rational analysis or let their emotions guide them

---

at the outset and subsequently looked for data or a rationale that supported their gut hunch.

How do we know when we are having a conflict between intellect and instinct?

Try to recollect a decision which was particularly difficult to make. Did you have a gut instinct about it? What did you feel? Where did you feel it in your body Think about how you make decisions: what methods do you use?

Emotions and Engagement

Emotions are the Secret to Engagement BUT 72%[12] of Organisations still don't get it!

Despite the fact that employee engagement is currently a significant issue for 91% of respondents (surveyed at the Learning and Skills Conference and Exhibition 28th and 29th Jan 2013, Olympia London) only 72% of organisations are aware of the difference between transactional and emotional engagement.

Until organisations understand the vital difference between being emotionally and transactionally engaged, businesses will

---

[12] Sample population: attendees at the Learning and Skills Exhibition 2013, Olympia London. Interviewed by The Maria Paviour Company.

fail to retain talent and achieve potential. The wrong kind of engagement can be undermining and dangerous to the business. Emotional engagement needs to be promoted within organisations with a view to improving working life for everyone; and profitability for the business.

It has been demonstrated in recent CIPD research that emotionally engaged employees perform better and are more likely to be retained.

Organisations need to start reviewing how their good intentions may be reducing emotional engagement; such as performance bonuses which are shown to have a negative effect on motivation and creativity. They need to review the way that middle managers manage (particularly the "mediocre" managers – who fly under the radar and according to CIPD research, do damage to the team); and begin modelling the kinds of 'A+B' behaviours in their leaders. It has to come from the top!

To become a great leader we need to recognise the qualities that are essential to credible leaders and organisations today and that starts with us understanding the concept of developing ourselves as leaders with EI as well as IQ. It's helpful to understand how our brain functions and learn to appreciate its importance.[13]

Emotional intelligence is fundamental to all relationships and when we appreciate the importance of 'gut feeling', and, indeed take a scientific view on this "gut feeling" we can improve our overall effectiveness as leaders. It also helps us to stay in control of our self.

"Leadership is almost all emotional intelligence, especially in distinguishing between what managers do and what leaders do..."

Mathew Juechter– chairman of ASTD

I find it easiest to focus on the four key pre-requisites of Emotional Intelligence and to consider these on the EI grid of happiness (that's my title, by the way). The reason I call it the grid of Happiness is 1) because I like the name – when something is happy it always sounds easier...2) because it makes the whole concept so easy to understand that you feel like skipping and clapping your hands with joy (ok maybe I'm

---

[13] Daniel Goleman

very easily pleased, but bear with me).

Emotional Intelligence Grid of Happiness

I like to make this bit as easy as possible, because, although EI is fantastic I think it is best as a measure of competence rather than a system of learning. My approach is more holistic. I suggest you don't get caught up on each of the individual competencies – but notice your improvement in them over time as you apply A+B Leadership principles.

THE EMOTIONAL INTELLIGENCE GRID OF HAPPINESS:

	SELF	SOCIAL
Recognition (mindfulness)	Self Awareness	Social Awareness
Regulation (empowerment)	Self Management	Relationship Management

5*Emotional Intelligence - after Daniel Goleman*

The following are components that are identified as being necessary for leaders. But as I say, use this to reflect back and not as a method for improvement. Too hard!

6 Components of Emotional Intelligence identified as necessary for leaders

EI Component	Definition
Innovation	Understanding your creative style coupled with the ability to generate creative responses to business problems yourself and through others.
Self-awareness	The ability to recognise and understand your moods, emotions, and drives, as well as their effect on others
Intuition	Using instinct, hunches, and feelings, along with facts and information to guide decisions
Self-regulation	The ability to control or redirect disruptive impulses and moods
	The propensity to suspend judgement, to think before acting
Motivation	A passion to work for reasons that go beyond money or status
	A propensity to pursue goals with energy and persistence
Empathy	The ability to understand the emotional makeup of other people
	Skill in treating people according to their emotional reactions
Social skill	Proficiency in managing relationships and building networks
	An ability to find common ground and build rapport

So referring back to the Grid of Happiness, notice that there are two things that you will have to learn (and, of course, these two things involve all manner of different elements, but more on that later).

1. **Mindfulness** – being aware of what you are doing, being aware in the moment. I'm not actually talking about the skill of Mindfulness in a meditative sense, although I think that has immense value, but I'm not a trained Mindfulness teacher. I'm talking about being mindful of what we say and do – noticing ourselves and the effect of our actions.

2. **Empowerment** – being able to make assertive choices about what we say and do, responding after we have employed some mindfulness, being able to state our needs.

How can EI support a leader to succeed?

What is the difference between a leader (e.g. helicopter view) and a manager (e.g. dealing with processes)? Is one more important than the other? Why? Ken Blanchard uses this metaphor for leaders and managers:

A path needed to be cleared through a rain-forest. A group of people began work. Progress was slow and haphazard until the manager organised people into teams of two-man saws.

Progress zipped along, but then the leader climbed to the top of the tree to observe. "Are we making progress?" asked the manager. "Yes we have gone a long way North," replied the leader, "but we want to go South!"[14]

The moral: To be effective you need a leader to steer and a manager to make progress effective.

Why does this Emotional Intelligence thing matter?

EI has been shown to predict performance in so many different industries from the US Airforce to L'Oreal, from office clerks to sales. High EI scores predict 127% more productive in their jobs, dramatically out-selling their lower EI scoring colleagues – in one case over twice as much. EI predicts better stress management, lower risk of your high EI staff leaving your company. High EI executives are more likely to perform in the top 1/3 of the company. High EI managers can reduce lost time accidents by 50%, reduce grievances in one case from 15% down to 30% per year. Even the most successful debt collectors have significantly greater EI than their less

---

[14] Blanchard, Kenneth H, and Spencer Johnson. The One Minute Manager. New York: Morrow, 1982. Print.

successful colleagues[15].[16]

Research has also shown that people prefer to deal with those people who have high EI.

So let's look at the key indicators of a happy and effective life, and how these are related to EI:

- You may get a job due to your IQ but you'll lose it with poor EI

- Delayed gratification, which is a function of being future-orientated (see Time Perspective, p.171) is a predictor of future career success, and also of better health and relationships.

- When we have good self-awareness we can create better relationships with other people, as we understand our needs. If we have good communication skills we can then explain our needs without resorting to manipulative or

---

[15] Bachman, J., Stein, S., Campbell, K., & Sitarenios, G. (2000). Emotional intelligence in the collection of debt. *International Journal of Selection and Assessment*, 8(3), 176-182.

[16] Spencer, L. M., Jr. , & Spencer, S. (1993). *Competence at work: Models for superior performance.* New York: John Wiley and Sons.

Spencer, L. M. J., McClelland, D. C., & Kelner, S. (1997). *Competency assessment methods: History and state of the art.* Boston: Hay/McBer.

Walter V. Clarke Associates. (1996). *Activity vector analysis: Some applications to the concept of emotional intelligence.* Pittsburgh, PA: Walter V. Clarke Associates.

controlling tactics. All in all, a nice healthy lifestyle with someone you love.

- As 40% of work absence is stress related the ability to manage our mental health has never been more important. Stress is about our perceptions of a situation and ability to judge its impact upon us, these are EI skills.[17]

- People with poor EI skills are more likely to lose their temper, react aggressively, get frustrated, lose attention and children may even become social outcasts.

I could go on, but instead I urge you to read everything you can on this, because the research is fascinating, and quite frankly, it's a no-brainer. [18]

---

[17] Hay/McBer Research and Innovation Group (1997). Reported in Daniel Goleman's book (Goleman, 1998).

Hunter, J. E., Schmidt, F. L., & Judiesch, M. K. (1990). Individual Differences in Output Variability as a Function of Job Complexity. *Journal of Applied Psychology*, 75, 28-42.

Lusch, R. F., & Serpkeuci, R. (1990). Personal differences, job tension, job outcomes, and store performance: A study of retail managers. *Journal of Marketing.*

McClelland, D. C. (1999). Identifying competencies with behavioral-event interviews. *Psychological Science*, 9(5), 331-339.

Pesuric, A., & Byham, W. (1996, July). The new look in behaviour modelling. *Training and Development*, 25-33.

[18] Business Case for Emotional Intelligence : Cary Cherniss 1999

Dr. Noelle Nelson, a clinical psychologist, trial consultant and author of "Make More Money by Making Your Employees Happy

You need good EI skills

It is clear that by ignoring the importance of emotions we are failing to tackle the first step in EI (self -awareness). By ignoring emotions we are denying the biochemical responses that we are programmed to have. Can you imagine the devastating effect this would have if we did this with anything else?

Can you imagine ignoring your thirst? What would happen if you just didn't drink because you refused to accept the message your body was giving you? Perhaps some kidney damage in the long term, in the short term, poor learning and tiredness (and smelly breath).

Just imagine you ignored a pain in your arm? This may be ok for a while, but would be foolish long term as it could be fatal – what if it was a heart attack?

Are women better leaders?

Some interesting research has shown that women are really finding their niche in the world of leadership. And in

Boyatzis, R. E. (1999). From a presentation to the Linkage Conference on Emotional Intelligence, Chicago, IL, September 27, 1999.

Boyatzis, R. (1982). *The competent manager: A model for effective performance*. New York: John Wiley and Sons.

Goleman, D. (1998). *Working with emotional intelligence*. New York: Bantam.

surprising ways. Women are perceived by their reports as being better leaders – and this is particularly interesting as men made up 78% of the leaders in the survey![19]

Furthermore, women tend to underestimate their abilities and men over estimate their abilities in leadership – when it comes to asking the people who follow them! And yet, it appears that there is bias against women in leadership roles simply because of stereotyping of gender. The stereotype of Woman just doesn't include leadership qualities. [20]

Let's allow Samantha, Lisa and David to have their say:

"Women are typically described and expected to be more communal, relations-oriented and nurturing than men, whereas men are believed and expected to be more agentic, assertive and independent than women... As organizations have become fast-paced, globalized environments, some organizational scholars have proposed that a more feminine style of

---

[19] Jack Zenger and Joseph Folkman, is based on a research study they did of 7,280 leaders in 2011.

[20] Paustian-Underdahl et al in APA's Journal of Applied Psychology®. Gender and perceptions of leadership Effectiveness: A meta-analysis of contextual moderators 2014

leadership is needed to emphasize the participative and open communication needed for success."

So you see, it's not me saying it, it comes from the research. And for this reason I've interviewed a number of leaders in business and communities who have been recommended to me – and it's no surprise given this research - that most of them are female.

CHAPTER 2

Secrets to Transactional or Emotional Engagement

Before I reveal all, we'll start with my background: I'm not an academic. I run a business, and I work with corporate organisations. I've studied psychology and biology. I really believe that communication is the foundation of all happiness in life - and success in business and life too. That's where I'm coming from: I like the positive psychology way of thinking about life.

Back in 1998 I won an EU award for my work in stress management. And then... I started noticing things. I noticed that there might be a bit of a connection between relationships and stress (not exactly going out on a limb here, am I!) which lead to me writing a book, *Changing Vampires into Angels - Six Steps to Heaven in Your Relationships*. And this started the process of me thinking about emotional engagement.

CASE STUDY: THE DEMON RISING

Now for more of my background - going back even further than when I did my degree (which is far enough!)

When I was seven, I was in a gang; The Treehouse Gang. There was me, and the two boys next door, Adrian and Nicholas. We used to get up to all sorts of adventures, and one day, Adrian and I decided that we were going to generate our very own myth: the demon rising. We thought the best way to generate it was with poor Nicholas, who was a year younger than us. So we said to him "Now, look Nicholas, today is the day that if you're *really* lucky, you'll see the demons rising on the other side of the corn field. But, first of all, you have to go and sit in the dark for half an hour."

So we kept Nicholas in the dark, and after a while rushed to the other side of the corn field. We painted our faces red, got dressed in the sort of attire a seven year old thinks a demon would wear (naturally plenty of red).

And then, at the appointed time, there he was - Nicholas, on the other side of the corn field. We jumped up and we danced

---

demonically, as we believed demons would dance - "Wooo! Oooo! Wooo!". Then we ducked down behind the corn, and crawled off into the woodland, desperately trying to take the paint off our faces while Nicholas was on the other side of the corn field shouting "Adrian, Maria, wait for me!"

At that point, I grew suspicious that Nicholas knew more than we thought; maybe he was a little bit doubtful of these demons!

In summary: As children it's easy to be emotionally engaged in pretty much anything. And we probably all have a story from our childhood just like that (well, maybe leaving out the demons bit, and the dancing...), where all of us were absorbed - even Nicholas, who was so emotionally engaged he even joined Adrian and me in it!

The efficient tightrope walker who pulled a sickie

You may be aware that there are two types of engagement - I'm going to expand now on what we mean by *emotionally* engaged. The other type of engagement, *transactional,* has been identified by the CIPD, and tends to be what people typically think of when talking about engagement - I know I used to. It's interesting - it's where you're really engaged in the job. But... It's a bit like being a tightrope walker: it can be highly stressful; and it can be highly dangerous. When you're transactionally engaged, you do get things done - it's about efficiency. One the other hand, transactionally engaged people sometimes pull sickies. They leave the company. There is a big difference between transactionally engaged employees, and emotionally engaged employees.[21]

The profit making footballer who kissed his badge

So *emotional* engagement - what's that all about? Well this here is Frank Lampard. Before you ask, no he's not wiping his nose! He's actually kissing his badge - his club badge. This is all about being engaged with the

organisation. Loving the organisation you work for. Emotional engagement has been shown to be the antithesis to stress - so whereas transactional

7 Image source: https://commons.wikimedia.org/wik i/File:Frank_Lampard_2010.JPG License: http://creativecommons.org/license s/by-sa/3.0/

---

[21] CIPD (May 2012) *CIPD: Emotional or transactional engagement – does it matter?* Kingston Engagement Consortium 23.05.12

engagement can be stressful, emotional engagement can actually be the solution to stress.

What's different about emotional engagement?

If you want to retain people, they need to be emotionally engaged. Because emotionally engaged people say "I love my company, I love my organisation, I love who I work for". Emotionally engaged people make a profit - they're effective. It's not so much about processing, but about people wanting to make a difference, because they believe in it.[22]

POP QUIZ! HOW EMOTIONALLY ENGAGED ARE YOU?

Here's a few questions to ask yourself… do you:

- Feel inspired by your work?
- Get so absorbed in your work that time flies and you forget everything around you?
- Want to go to work in the mornings
- Wake up on a Monday morning going "yay!"
- Feel a sense of pride in your work?
- Become energetic at work?
- Feel happy working really intensely?

---

[22] Sinek, Simon. *Start With Why*. New York: Portfolio, 2009. Print..

> These are some of the pointers of emotional engagement - the more yes, the better!

Is the coffee *really* that bad?

I spoke with a client recently who had attended a forum on engagement surveys, with some really big players - supermarket chains and more. They all had the same question: "why is it that we get hammered on the pay and rewards question? We pay people pretty well, why do we get a bad score on pay and rewards?" One of the people at the forum suggested that actually, people just need to vent. It's not really pay and rewards that's the problem. So they thought "Well, maybe we should keep the question in there, to give people the opportunity to vent." And I asked myself: what is the point of that? You need to know what is *really* going on. Not to have a venting question that actually covers up the problem! This is one of the dangers if you're doing an engagement survey - be careful, and ensure that you're looking at the emotional undercurrent as well. It's what I call 'The Coffee Machine Scenario' - if people complain about the coffee, it often means that there's something else entirely that's the problem. We're not always upset for the reasons we think we are!

So, why does this venting happen? If you ask cognitive questions about emotional responses, you may get rationalised answers. This is because the structures in the brain that register emotions, don't have any capacity for language. And when you're the one answering a survey, saying "It doesn't feel right" doesn't really stack up - it's not good enough for a survey! So we have to rationalise how we're feeling. So when the survey analysis comes along, it's imperative that we as survey developers look at both cognitive *and* emotional responses. That's the challenge for us.

When people complain about the coffee they may be saying much more….

I often work with businesses who have carried out staff surveys and who are carefully implementing the outcome's the recommendations. Sometimes these can fall by the wayside, though, when they do not appear to be creating the huge rush of appreciation and motivation that is expected from the employees! They ask me "why isn't this working?"

Don't be surprised!

The things that dissatisfy (known as hygiene factors) will always cause low morale. We know that these are *not* motivators, but that until they are removed people will not respond and be positively motivated. So, sources of dissatisfaction need to be removed first. After all, a freezing cold office is very de-motivating, but a nice warm office is hardly motivating! I don't think to myself, I can't wait to get to work because my office is such a lovely temperature!

However, unless dealing with these hygiene factors is combined with factors that *motivate* it will not improve staff morale. It seems a little unfair, but the fact is the removal of dissatisfiers is a vital pre-requisite, but not in itself enough to alter staff attitude.

By the same token, no matter how much good work you do on motivating people, it will not make a difference unless the dissatisfiers are removed.[23]

We know that the part of the brain that deals with emotions has no language and so therefore we can find it difficult to find the right words when we express emotions. If people are voicing dissatisfaction it may be that they are "rationalising" emotional responses by attaching their feelings to a hygiene factor. For example, they may be complaining about meeting rooms because they feel negative about meetings, or under pressure etc. They may complain about the coffee machine,

---

[23] Herzberg, F. The Motivation to Work 1959 ISBN-13: 978-1560006343

when they are really complaining about the lack of appreciation they feel.

People frequently create a label for how they are feeling that ostensibly appears to be rational – in order to give credence to "non-rational" emotions.

It's important to add that because an emotion cannot be given a rational explanation, it does not mean that it is not valid – both in terms of the individual and in terms of the information it provides to the business. Emotions are our most basic survival mechanism, and not paying heed to them can be disastrous – in business and life.

So think in terms of removing dissatisfiers first and foremost, and only then consider how to provide the right environment in which your people can feel motivated and engaged.

The measures of emotional engagement

1) Vigour; the physicality. How do people put their bodies into their work? How do they invest their physical energy?
2) Dedication: about the emotional
3) Absorption: which is about cognition[2425]

---

[24] Schaufeli, Wilmar B. et al. 'Journal Search Results - Cite This For Me'. Journal of Happiness Studies 3.1 (2002): 71-92. Web.
http://www.wilmarschaufeli.nl/publications/Schaufeli/178.pdf

Measure 1: Vigour

This relates to resilience, energy, and being mentally strong. If you want energetic people, who persevere through difficulties, who love applying themselves enthusiastically and wholeheartedly to their work, they need to have really healthy levels of self-efficacy. A belief in their abilities, in their capabilities to achieve a goal or an outcome. It's that belief: *I can do it*. That's really important.

And it's important to everyone, from all walks of life - and as with everything, isn't something you can stereotype. I've done work recently with a large telecoms company, who employ lots of engineers. We did a little pilot programme with them on self-empowerment, which we thought might appeal to a lot of women in the organisation. And 80% of those who signed up were men.

Self-efficacy, the need for self-empowerment, is vital to emotional engagement. Because if you don't believe you can make a difference within yourself, you can't become emotionally engaged with your organisation.

---

[25] The Utrecht engagement scale – defined and © by Utrecht University is based on these factors

Measure 2: Dedication

This is the desire to invest emotionally in the work; it's about meaning, purpose, inspiration, and pride. What we're talking about is value - and not the corporate big boys of (big shouty voice) "We have values of INTEGRITY, and we have values of CUSTOMER SERVICE, you KNOW we do because they're on our WEBSITE!" I don't mean that. I mean what *really* matters here. What really matters to us.

Back to the future of engagement

You can see a great example if you go back in time, to Anita Roddick and The Body Shop. The values were in everything they did - they just spoke values. And it's because it was all about meaning something to people. It's coming back to the people in the teams, working with them, looking at, what's their emotional commitment to this? How do they feel about being emotionally engaged with our organisation? Can we align our values with them?

Lining up values and behaviours

The Body Shop takes this very seriously. And they should - we all should - because it is really important. Our beliefs are fundamental to our sense of self - what is important to us is fundamental to who we are. And when our values are out of line with our behaviours, then it screws us up. On a lighter note, you could call it cognitive dissonance! It causes a real problem for people - it creates severe mental disturbance. So if the values and the behaviours they're putting into their work don't line up, something's going to give. They're either going to go somewhere else where they feel that they can express their values, or something else is going to happen.

Sabotage!

When people find themselves not feeling like they can really express their values, things can start to go wrong. People may start doing things that can harm the organisation. That sounds quite a big deal - harming the organisation - you immediately think, "Sabotage!". Harming the organisation is things like being rude to a customer. Maybe being a little bit generous to yourself on your expenses. It's that sense of not really caring sufficiently about the organisation: "I don't really love the organisation enough for it to matter to me." So values are *really* important, and they need to be values that resonate: "Something that I can feel part of."

CASE STUDY

INFORMATION GOVERNANCE IN THE NHS

Now doesn't that sound exciting! And that was the problem: I did an interesting piece of work with the NHS, on information governance, and there was total disengagement from all employees. Not the sexiest topic ever!

So, we started looking at what it was really all about: why were we doing these things? How were they benefitting patients? How were they benefitting the people who worked there? How were they ensuring that we could continue to run the business, even if things went wrong?

And we realised that when people became really engaged in the purpose, the reason for it, they totally got it.

An auditor came round and said "Can you tell me where the emergency drawer is for when you have emergency downtime?" (this is when the computers go down, and everything can go really wrong in terms of patient records). Every member of staff said "It's in that drawer there" and the auditor went and looked in the drawer, and said "There's nothing here." And they said, "No, we're using it!"

And this is the thing: it was constantly being used. The auditor came away and said "This is gold standard. This isn't just policy, this is policy in action - these people are completely committed to this."

Well yes - because they got it! And this is why values are so important.

Measure 3: Absorption

And the next thing which is fundamental - particularly to me - is that you need to design for happiness. This is really interesting - a positive psychologist Mihaly Csikszentmihalyi (pronounced Me-Hi, Cheek-Sent-Me-Hi) has done some work on a form of happiness. There are basically three forms of happiness, and this is one of them: it is called *flow*.

The Skills/Challenge Balance: flow[26]

His idea is that if you can hit that sweet point between skills and challenge - enough skills being used, and sufficient challenge - you get into something called flow. Now, I don't know if you've ever had this experience - being so involved in something that you've lost all sense of time and space, and it's

---

[26] Csikszentmihalyi, Mihaly. *Good Business*. New York: Viking, 2003. Print.

just happened? And you've been fantastically creative. My son is a scriptwriter, he says that sometimes he is so immersed in what he's doing, he's working so much at his level of bliss, that actually he isn't writing - he's taking dictation from the characters in his film. They are speaking to him, they are telling him the story. They are taking him down whatever path they're going to go - he doesn't know! That is what flow is like. Some people call it a spiritual experience. But it's actually a cognitive process that is going on. If you're going to design for happiness, then design for flow. You need to make sure you've got learning of skills, goals, and feedback built in. There needs to be autonomy; they need to have some control, and they need to be able to concentrate and be involved.[27]

So you're wandering about the others forms of happiness now, aren't you?

They all have a place in work. In different ways...

Pleasant Life - Happiness

This is the happiness we get from going out and doing great things, buying nice stuff etc. At work we get this from having

---

[27] Karasek, R., & Theorell, T. (1990) Healthy Work: Stress, Productivity and the Reconstruction of Working Life. Basic Books, New York. The degree of control over work is a factor in health at work. The more control the healthier the individual.

a laugh with people and getting a promotion. It is often the form we seek, but it is also the form that has the least durability. We know that lottery winners may think they will be as happy as can be forever more, but actually, when you measure their happiness, and the unhappiness of people who become severely disabled, it appears that, yes lottery winners are amazingly happy – and who become disabled are unhappy – but amazingly, after 6 months their happiness generally evens out! This is due to our ability to synthesise happiness. It seems that happiness comes from the inside after all – and that we can create happiness in the way we view the world and ourselves in it! [28]

Happiness in Service

Now, what was I saying about information governance? Well this form of happiness, the happiness we derive from serving others is the most enduring of all. As leaders, if we can align our values with our actions and make a business that serves, we will be able to create happiness for ourselves, even more than the ones we serve! [29]

All about the money?

---

[28] Gilbert, D. (2007). *Stumbling on happiness*. London: Harper Perennial.

[29] Martin Seligman ISBN-13: 9780743222983

There's a great book - Dan Pink's[30] round up on the research of motivations. He talks about what really motivates people, and it's not money. And we know this, research proves it. But... hot off the press: HSBC are increasing their bonuses, but they are reducing their holiday. Even when there's enough money on the table, you still need the other factors I've talked about to gain real emotional engagement. Intrinsic motivation teaches us it's not about money. And it's interesting to realise that bonuses crush creativity and reduce performance. In fact, the bigger the bonus, the worse the performance. I think somebody needs to talk to the banks! So, if you want to retain talent, which is what these people often say, lets remind them of what Lennon and McCartney say: money can't buy you love. Right?

Happiness is a business solution!

I've been running a course for years called Happiness AS a Business Solution - I've renamed it Happiness IS a Business Solution!

This is the thing about happiness:

- 31% improved performance in people who are happy

---

[30] Pink, Daniel H. *Drive - the surprising truth about what motivates us.* Edinburgh: Canongate, 2010. Print.

- 37% improvement in sales, when sales people are happy

- 18% improved speed and accuracy of diagnosis in Drs who are happy

I apologised to a doctor colleague of mine- I felt kind of guilty about it only being 18%, not 37%. And he said "Hey look, that's nearly a fifth better, come on - that's life saving stuff!"[31]

Travelling over the cognitive horizon

The thing with happiness is that we often push it over the cognitive horizon - I'll be happy when... ever say that? Or, I'll relax when... It'll be ok when... I'll feel better when... and it's actually a way of travelling - it's about being happy in the now. It's really important for gaining emotional commitment from people - and emotional engagement.

The other thing is personal empowerment - we need to have the sense of self-efficacy. We need to be able to know that we can make a difference.

Emotional engagement underminers

If you want to get people emotionally engaged, start with the line managers. Recent research[32] has shown that mediocre line

---

[31] Achor, Shawn. *The Happiness Advantage*. New York: Broadway Books, 2010. Print.

managers are the real problem in organisations, because they fly under the radar. We know who are the poor ones, and we know who are the top fliers. But the ones in the middle... Start with line manager relationships - that is vital in ensuring you get emotional commitment in your teams. It is also important to know that it's been shown that organisational structure can really undermine emotional engagement.

Leadership and management development are a priority, but skills are definitely lacking in middle managers.[33] Are your organisation structures supporting emotional engagement, or are they undermining it? And leadership can be the main cause of loss of trust - it can undermine trust.[34]

---

[32] CIPD: *Perspectives on Leadership 2012: Implications for HR*. Lewis and Donaldson-Feilder 10.09.12

[33] http://www.peoplemanagement.co.uk/pm/articles/2013/02/leadership-research-reveals-managers-struggle-with-basic-skills.htm?utm_medium=email&utm_source=cipd&utm_campaign=pmdaily&utm_content=1 20213_news_1 11 February 2013

[34] Hope-Hailey, Veronica, Ros Searle, and Graham Dietz. *Where Has All The Trust Gone?* CIPD, 2012. Web. 7 Sept. 2015. Stewardship, Leadership, Governance.

EMOTIONAL ENGAGEMENT AND ME

My story of how I entered the world of engagement doesn't end in 2002, when I wrote *Changing Vampires into Angels*. In 2004 I had a head injury. I was unable to work for two years. That was tough. And I was unable to take my daughter to her first day at school. That was tougher. I lost a lot of my speech, my gestures, my short-term memory, and my ability to cope with sensory stimulation. Like, for example, shopping - of all things! Just going into the supermarket was a mind killer. So I wasn't able to continue my high life of global travel unfortunately! So I gained a local contract. And the chap that I contracted with had values and ethics that I completely aligned to. And I discovered, that from being this slightly vegetative person who could barely walk down the stairs to get a cup of tea, suddenly I had boundless energy - and I could do all the stuff I loved doing! I had a purpose here, that I believed in, and I was able to perform at exceptional levels cognitively. This was a complete surprise to my neuropsychologist, who had tested me previously and I couldn't do even very basic things - it made a huge difference.

This should be a really happy ending. But it's not. It became very apparent that there was some very serious wrongdoing that others were involved in. And I became a whistle-blower.

Kim Holt, the whistle-blower in the tragic Baby P case is now the leader of the whistle-blower's charity, Patients First. She shared this with me: no one can even imagine the bullying of whistle-blowers, unless they've experienced it themselves. And I agree. After the bullying comes anxiety, deep dark moods, and a complete sense of disengagement. Not just in work, but in life.

So what did I do? I reinvented my business. I decided I would structure for emotional engagement, for flow and happiness. I got into my bliss, and I started to do what really mattered, what really matters to me. I got back to basics: self-confidence, self-esteem. I acknowledged my emotions, other peoples' emotions, and the effect my emotions were having on other people, as well as theirs on me.

Improving profit, curing ills

We are living in times of economic uncertainty, debt, corporate scandal, so called people of standing preying on the vulnerable getting away with murder, or at least abuse. There is an upsurge in attitudes of entitlement, not only in employees, but also business leaders. And so much stock being placed in money, bonuses being the measure of work - but not always competence and talent. Knowing that only 1-3% of people in the population are naturally everyday heroes[35] who will stand up to wrongdoing, and that another 1% are probably psychopaths[36]. In these days when strong ethics and values are paramount, emotional engagement has never been more important! Emotional engagement is not only the cure to all your business ills, and the answer to improved profit. Emotion engages people. And emotionally engaged people, save lives.

And an end note: how do you engender compassion, honesty, passion and respect in the workplace? Well emotional engagement will do that. But if you're going to have that then you have to come in with a positive attitude to *vulnerability*. Why? Because compassion responds to it. Honesty requires it, and passion exposes it.

So, this is what is required of you to engender emotional engagement at work: your courage. You have to step into your own vulnerability on this. You know, we're talking *emotions* here. Your trust in your people as well as yourself - in all your

---

[35] Zimbardo, P (2008) *The Lucifer Effect: how good people turn evil* Rider; paperback / softback edition (6 Mar. 2008) ISBN 1846041031

[36] Hare, Robert D. Without Conscience. New York: Guilford Press, 1999. Print.

people. And your universal acceptance of vulnerability in everyone.

A few years ago I used to say love was the only four letter word you can't use in the boardroom. Actually, today, it's vulnerability that people don't want to talk about. Without vulnerability, to quote Rene Brown, we can't have innovation, change and creativity.

So to end this chapter, I want you to remember the story of me with my three little friends, and remember that we all have within us that childlike ability to become completely emotionally engaged in what we do, and that we have the ability to find the fun and the purpose in absolutely anything, and put our heart and soul into it. And if we remember that emotions connect us, then let's get out there, shake hands with the person next to us, step into our vulnerability, and let's make some good connections.

"Brainy" Neuroscience for Engaged People

CHAPTER 3
What's getting in the way of
engagement? Is it you?

N ow, we're going to explore the barriers to emotional
engagement, and how much they will cost you, and
what return on investment you could get for removing them.
And I'm not just going to make you read and read and read
and then say, "You know what, it costs A LOT, and your
return on investment could be really BIG." I will actually give
you real figures, based on CIPD and government backed
evidence (you can always skip ahead to find out, but then
you'll miss what the barriers are!)

The wellbeing activist

I've been pushing wellbeing - even when it wasn't a top priority for organisations - for a long time now. One of the things I can tell you after years working and researching in this field, is that you cannot improve emotional engagement until you have eliminated the barriers - you *have* to do that first. There is one vast and terrifying barrier, which is costing organisations millions of pounds simply because we haven't noticed it. Millions of pounds! Or haven't we?

How do you know there's an elephant in your fridge?

Which takes me off on a tangent. When I was about seven years old, my father had a precision engineering company. He was advanced in ideas on wellbeing at work, and keen on the idea of work life balance. He would have business meetings in restaurants over dinner, and the whole family would go - so I was out there, seeing his clients. And because these clients knew that I had a bit of a thing about elephant jokes, they would indulge me and say "Do you know any new elephant jokes Maria?" and of course, I would resist! Hmm, well maybe not! Eventually being persuaded to tell jokes like "How do you know if an elephant is in bed with you? It's the letter 'E' on his pyjamas!" And "What did the man say when he saw three elephants coming over the hill? Oh look, there are 3 elephants coming over the hill." And then "What did the man say when he saw three elephants coming over the hill wearing sunglasses? He didn't say anything because he didn't recognise them!"

The thing about elephant jokes, is that really they are elephant in the room jokes. Because what they are talking about really is the fact that it is so obvious it is staring you in the face. So when I say we haven't noticed this vast barrier to emotional

8 *Elephant in disguise by Jazz*

engagement, what I'm actually saying is it could well be the elephant in the room. And that maybe, when we do notice it, we're not doing anything about it.

Stand up, sit down, keep moving

At this point, I'm going to tell you to put this book down and MOVE. Get up, and if there's anyone near you, bump fists with them and tell them something you really love. Get them to do the same to you. Do it with as many people as you can, in the next 30 seconds. The rule is that you can't repeat anything, or duplicate what anyone else has said. GO!

Usually, I do this with a group of people, in person. And it makes a point beautifully for me. You feel different right? I could get a Doctor to test your blood, saliva and urine, and they would *prove* that you feel different. This is because you just changed your body chemistry. This works fantastically for me, because now you are energised. So I have an energised reader, an involved reader! Transferring this to the world of work: if you were a manager/leader, and your team were energised, you would emotionally respond to this, and in turn would become more energised, and so an engagement schema forms. This is partly the answer to emotional engagement. But there is an awful lot more to it than that...

Body, heart and mind

If you want people to be emotionally engaged, they have to make an investment, in three things: body, heart and mind. They need to invest physical energy. There has to be commitment emotionally - if you're going to be emotionally engaged, you have to be committed emotionally. And the mind - there has to be challenge, they have to feel they can challenge themselves and that they can master skills. So the journey is physical, emotional, and cognitive. Engagement is the positive antithesis burn out. [37]

The Ape and the Golden Retriever

---

[37] Maslach, C., Schaufeli, W. and Leiter, M. (2001). *Job Burnout.* Annual Review of Psychology, 52(1), pp.397-422.

Before we go further, I'm going to clarify the difference between being *transactionally* and *emotionally* engaged. Before we can understand the barriers, we must understand this difference. So, in the picture we have a lovely little transactionally engaged ape. And a lovely golden retriever, who is demonstrating emotional commitment. And the difference? The retriever is doing it for love, he's part of a family. The ape just has to do it. Transactionally engaged people feel much more stress than emotionally engaged people. Emotionally engaged people tend not to feel stress, they tend to be energised. There is an important message here for organisations: engagement not just about how you feel, but about how well you perform. [38]

We want lockers and coffee!

So harking back to what I was saying earlier about what motivates us, let us consider the engagement survey. I'm sure if you're involved in these, you will have noticed this: one of the things people often complain about is pay and conditions. "We're not engaged because we're not paid enough". And probably, you know that conditions and pay are not motivators

---

[38] Engaged employees become physically involved in their tasks, cognitively alert and emotionally connected to others when performing their job. In contrast, disengaged employees become disconnected from their jobs, and hide their true identity, thoughts and feelings during role performances (Olivier & Rothermann 2007)

- that's old news. As Dan Pink says, there is a big difference between what science knows and what business does. When people say to you in those surveys that pay and rewards are the problem, what they are really saying is "You don't care". And when they're saying the problem is the coffee machine, or lack of lockers, they're actually saying "You don't care enough about me to give me a decent cup of coffee", or "You don't care enough about me to look after my things that mean something to me". If it wasn't that, then the highest paid people in the world would be the most engaged. If that was true, then why do banks offer huge amounts of money to retain staff? The staff should all be in love with the banks, surely? So, highest paid is not an indicator of engagement.

Going incognito

Undercover Boss - a documentary programme on Channel 4 in the UK[39]. The premise is that the 'boss' of a large organisation goes 'undercover', back to the shop floor, and works with his employees on the front line to get a taste and feel for how the business works in reality, and the state of engagement.

I watched "Undercover Boss" on the television in which the boss of Carluccio's – the Italian restaurant chain that is

---

[39] 'Carluccio's' (2014) *Undercover Boss,* Series 6, Episode 6, Channel 4, 20th August

looking to expand dramatically – disguised himself as a budding entrepreneur who was making a documentary about starting up his own business. Under this pretence he went undercover to see what was happening in his restaurants; in particular, whether his employees were delivering.

Of course, careful editing may affect my perception but in any event I was struck by the quality of the staff – their energy and dedication to customer service was (from what I could see) excellent; the waiter really engaged with his customers, the barista was really keen on providing fantastic coffee.

An aspiring Sous Chef had been left in charge for the kitchen for three months, with no training, no Head Chef and no General Manager – the boss observed that the restaurant was not tidy and clean enough... well not exactly a surprise under the circumstances.

The problem they all revealed was that they felt management didn't really care, didn't notice them, didn't listen to them - basically that management and leadership were on a cloud somewhere.

BUT the staff also shared with the disguised boss that they felt undervalued and "like a number". The company had not recognised and rewarded their hard work.

The Chief Executive, Simon Kossoff, came back from his undercover trip, and said it was a problem with staff morale.

Morale? Really?

I understand his concern, but I say no, it wasn't. It's not a problem of staff morale. If your people are performing *in spite of* the business, it's not a problem of staff morale, it's a problem of what is going on behind that. It is a problem of what is going on in management. This may seem a bit of a moot point, but it's important.

I'm not pointing the finger at first line managers - they do the most difficult of all management jobs. I'm saying that they are the ones that need to be supported. If your people at the coal face are not being able to perform, it is management that is the problem. But it's not the individual, it's not a problem of staff morale - their morale is fine, if you look after them a bit. They're doing the job.

I'm really impressed with Simon Kossoff having the courage to find out what is really going on in the business. And I'm convinced that Carluccio's will only be better as a result of his dedication to listen and act.

Morale rarely is the problem.

It makes me feel fidgety when I see great staff delivering at a high standard and then hear that morale is a problem – quite obviously the staff are perfectly capable of delivering, so it is not their morale that is the problem, it is the failure of management to support them. To put it another way, would the staff be feeling low if they had been acknowledged, rewarded or supported? Answer is clearly "no". They feel low but they soldier on... so I say "leave the staff alone, they are not the problem, and go sort out the managers!" (not one of which appeared on screen).

The most important trust relationship at work is between employee and line manager – if this is broken then nothing else works – it doesn't matter how great head office staff are, this is the relationship that will make or break your business.

We all love lovely things!

Simon Kossoff wanted to show that he really did care about his staff and so he told them he was going to close the café for a day and give them all a party. And a party is what I call a 'lovely thing'. And there are lots of lovely things that you

9: Badger Party, by Tate

can do in business. Employee of the month, bonuses, family picnics, bring your dog to work day, foosball, staff canteen… BUT all the lovely things in the world will not amount to anything in terms of emotional engagement unless you've eliminated the barriers - and I still haven't told you what that big one is!

A disillusioned waiter may be delighted when he is promised by the Boss that his restaurant would close one day for a big party. In that moment he would feel appreciated. However, when all the balloons have gone down, the loud music is a distant memory and he is faced with a Manager who doesn't know how to value him, will he still feel as good? So the party is not enough on its own – as Kossoff was aware – and he set about tackling other areas to ensure his staff would have a more sustainable, long term improvement in their morale and engagement levels.

This is not a criticism of lovely things. Not at all. I love them as much as anyone else. And I certainly support Kossoff's refreshingly open-handed and open-minded approach to his people. That is the most engaging thing of all.

Lovely things and engagement

Recently Virgin totally changed their holiday policy. Holiday is not tracked, staff can take as much as they want. Will it make any difference to engagement? Well, the question is, are the people already engaged? With Virgin it is likely to work, because they already have a very good engagement score. When Virgin do a lovely thing, it will make a difference. So, lovely things are fantastic, because they show you care, but they can't be there in place of the most important things that show you care - they've got to be there first. Emotional engagement responds to how much you care.

My Wellbeing at Work Formula:

$$WB@W = R + WP$$

(Wellbeing at Work is equal to
Relationships plus Work Pressure)

But it's not as straightforward as that, because relationships and work pressure are not equally impactful. It's actually:

$$WB@W = 3R + WP$$

In other words, if Work Pressure is negative (however you perceive that) but Relationships are good, then Wellbeing is likely to be good. But if Work Pressure is not a problem, and Relationships are poor, Wellbeing is likely to be poor. Relationships are the factor. This is scientifically based research, this isn't just making it up! This is how it works: relationships are vital. [40] Work engagement helps individuals deal with the demands of stressful work [41] and has been shown to be positively related to organisational commitment[42] and employee performance [43]

Our personal experience of stress, in terms of our behaviours, our psychology and physiological responses will affect the way in which we cope and deal with work demands. [44]

---

[40] Exploring positive relationships at work: Building a theoretical and research foundation. LEA's organization and management series. Dutton, Jane E. (Ed); Ragins, Belle Rose (Ed) Mahwah, NJ, US: Lawrence Erlbaum Associates Publishers *Exploring positive relationships at work: Building a theoretical and research foundation*. (2007). xxi 421 pp.

[41] Britt, T., Adler, A. and Bartone, P. (2001). *Deriving benefits from stressful events: The role of engagement in meaningful work and hardiness.* Journal of Occupational Health Psychology, 6(1), pp.53-63.

[42] Demerouti, E., Bakker, A., de Jonge, J., Janssen, P. and Schaufeli, W. (2001). *Burnout and engagement at work as a function of demands and control.* Scandinavian Journal of Work, Environment & Health, 27(4), pp.279-286.

[43] Aktour, O. (1992). Management And Theories Of Organizations In The 1990s: Toward A Critical Radical Humanism?. *Academy of Management Review*, 17(3), pp.407-431.

[44] Levi, L. (1984) *Stress in Industry: Causes, Effects and Prevention.* Occupational Safety and Health Series no. 51, International Labour Office, Geneva.

The importance of a situation is a key and defining factor in the intensity of our response, and therefore the impact of stress. [45]

There is a plethora of research that supports the power effective relationships have on stress and coping. A survey by the Ministry of Labour in Japan (1987) revealed that 52% of the women interviewed had experienced anxiety and stress, the main cause being unsatisfactory interpersonal relations at work (61%). Similarly, Jones et al. (1998) found that workers reporting high levels of stress and stress-related illnesses were 6 times more likely to report "lack of support from people in charge at work" than the general working population.

The key relationships that have impactful affects are:

- superiors
- subordinates
- colleagues

Low interpersonal support at work has been found to be associated with **high anxiety, emotional exhaustion**, job

---

[45] Lazarus, R.S. & Folkman, S. (1984). *Stress, Appraisal and Coping.* Springer Publications, New York .

tension, low job satisfaction and increased risk of cardiovascular disease [46]

Research suggests that where social relationships are strong this moderates the effect of stress, and that where they are poor the effects of stress are greater. A study of Swedish male workers showed that supportive colleagues and supervisors

---

[46] BEEHR, T. and NEWMAN, J. (1978). Job Stress, Employee Health, And Organizational Effectiveness: A Facet Analysis, Model, And Literature Review. *Personnel Psychology*, 31(4), pp.665-699.

Davidson, M. and Cooper, C. (1981). A Model of Occupational Stress. *Journal of Occupational Health and Environmental Medicine Journal of Occupational Medicine*, 23(8), pp.564-574.

Warr, P. (1992). Age and occupational well-being. Psychology and Aging, 7(1), pp.37-45.

Tennant, C. (2001). Work-related stress and depressive disorders. *Journal of Psychosomatic Research*, 51(5), pp.697-704.

Sarason, I., Sarason, B. and Pierce, G. (1990). Social Support: The Search for Theory. *Journal of Social and Clinical Psychology*, 9(1), pp.133-147.

Impact Factor:1.832 | Ranking:Public, Environmental & Occupational Health (SSCI) 50 out of 145 | Public, Environmental & Occupational Health (SCI) 73 out of 162 Source:2014 Journal Citation Reports® (Thomson Reuters, 2015)

Hardy, J. and Smith, T. (1988). Cynical hostility and vulnerability to disease: Social support, life stress, and physiological response to conflict. *Health Psychology*, 7(5), pp.447-459.

Magnusson Hanson, L., Theorell, T., Oxenstierna, G., Hyde, M. and Westerlund, H. (2008). Demand, control and social climate as predictors of emotional exhaustion symptoms in working Swedish men and women. *Scandinavian Journal of Public Health*, 36(7), pp.737-743.

Magnusson Hanson, L., Theorell, T., Oxenstierna, G., Hyde, M. and Westerlund, H. (2008). Demand, control and social climate as predictors of emotional exhaustion symptoms in working Swedish men and women. *Scandinavian Journal of Public Health*, 36(7), pp.737-743.

reduced depression and job satisfaction caused by job demands.

A recent meta-analytical study of 68 previous papers

confirmed the presence of three general constructs (stressors, strains and social support). Their results indicated Social support reduced the strains experienced,

10 Grateful Gerald
By Jazz

social support mitigated perceived stressors, and social support moderated the stressor–strain relationship. [47]

Although there is a direct link between the number of hours worked and stress levels, the number of hours worked was positively related to the perceived availability of social support.[48][49]

---

[47] Viswesvaran, C., Sanchez, J. and Fisher, J. (1999). *The Role of Social Support in the Process of Work Stress: A Meta-Analysis.* Journal of Vocational Behavior, 54(2), pp.314-334.

[48] Fielden, S. and Peckar, C. (1999). *Work stress and hospital doctors: a comparative study.* Stress Medicine, 15(3), pp.137-141.

[49] Cox, T, Griffiths, A, Rial-González, E. The European Agency for Safety and Health at Work, (2000). *Research on work-related stress.* Office for Official Publications of the European Communities, 2000.

What do we want from our colleagues?

What do we have to do to make relationships really supportive? Ok, have a think about this: what do we want from the people we work with?

- Somebody who will listen to us, to our new ideas?
- Somebody we can rely on?
- Somebody who's sociable, who will walk into the office and say hello?
- Somebody who is compassionate, caring, helpful?
- Somebody quite stable, emotionally speaking? Who won't chuck their toys out of the pram every five minutes?

In psychology terms, these traits describe 'The Big Five'[50]

The Big Five - aka OCEAN

These are the key positive, the adaptive traits we look for, summed up by the acronym OCEAN[51].

*11 Lil' Fishy Guy
By Jazz*

- Openness: open to experience - someone who will listen
- Conscientiousness: someone to rely on

---

[50] Costa, P.T.,Jr. & McCrae, R.R. (1992). *Revised NEO Personality Inventory (NEO-PI-R) and NEO Five-Factor Inventory (NEO-FFI) manual.* Odessa, FL: Psychological Assessment Resources.

[51] Buss, D. M. (1995). *Evolutionary psychology: A new paradigm for psychological science.* Psychological Inquiry, 6, 1-31.

- Extraversion: someone who's outgoing enough to communicate with you

- Agreeableness: people who are compassionate, caring and helpful

- Neuroticism: this tends to be called 'emotional stability' now, but neuroticism is the scale - so, someone who tends to be more emotionally stable[52]

But what about people who don't have those traits? In "The Bad Seed" by William March the woman who is stressed, drinking and emotionally out of control and therefore appears "mad" is actually the victim of a psychopath. And the psychopath is...a child, Rhoda Penmark[53]. The image shows Ingrid Bergman, in the film Gaslight[54] - from which the

12Charles Boyer, Ingrid Bergman: Gaslight 1944

---

[52] McCrae, R.R., & Costa, P.T. (1987) *Validation of the five-factor model of personality across instruments and observers.* Journal of Personality and Social Psychology, 52, 81-90.

McCrae, R.R., & Costa, P.T. (1997) *Personality trait structure as a human universal.* American Psychologist, 52, 509-516.

[53] *The Bad Seed* (1956) Directed by Mervyn LeRoy [film], USA: Warner Brothers

[54] *Gaslight* (1944) Directed by George Cukor [Film], USA: Metro-Goldwyn-Meyer

the term was coined: 'gaslighting', where people are driven mad by small, incremental changes so that they begin to doubt their own sanity. Ingrid's husband convinces her that she is weak in the mind, and when she discovers the truth she gets quite angry. As you probably can imagine.

The thing is, that anger, that emotional response – completely natural of course - can also be used against the victim.

Who's a psychopath really?

Dr Robert Hare, the world leading expert on psychopathy, has an internet forum for victims called Aftermath[55]. And this is the sort of thing people say there: "If you shout out that someone is a psychopath, you are the one they all call mad and unreasonable. Then the psychopath says 'there you are, see what madness I have to deal with?'" This is what Babiack and Hare[56] call 'snakes in suits'. And if someone reacts like this it doesn't necessarily mean they are unstable - because actually this can be a normal reaction. Being unemotional is abnormal.

---

[55] Hare, R. (1999). *Without conscience.* New York: Guilford Press.

[56] Babiak, P. and Hare, R. (2006). *Snakes in suits.* New York: Regan Books.

The Dark Triad

So, your worst case scenario in terms of barriers to engagement? The Dark Triad: psychopaths, narcissists, Machiavellianists. These are at worst your elephant sized barrier. Psychopaths are selfish, callous, and remorseless. Narcissism, in a nutshell, is manipulative behaviours. Machiavellianism is secretive, deceptive. This information does all come with a caveat: don't now go out and diagnose everyone with personality disorders! You do need to be aware that this is one end of the spectrum of behaviour, the extreme end, and that there are some people who have these personality disorders. But only 1 person in 100 is a psychopath. And a lot of them are locked up! So in your career, you may come across this maybe a couple of times, maybe more. The key thing here is: we don't tend to look at it - we look away.

Hunting out the negative

Nigel Guenole published a paper, *Maladaptive Personalities at Work - Exploring the Darkness*[57]. In it, he states that the problem is we're not looking for these traits in business. We're so busy looking for the positives, that no-one is saying, "You

---

[57] Guenole, N. (2014). Maladaptive Personality at Work: Exploring the Darkness. Industrial and Organizational Psychology, 7(1), pp.85-97.

know what, we actually also have to be aware of things that are *not* right". It's very difficult to do this, because when someone is helping you (even if you don't want them to), or someone is so beloved and adored by everyone, but you feel that they manipulated, lied and betrayed your trust, when you have been "gas lit", it is difficult.

The Psychopath's Bubble

So you have to be aware that The Dark Triad contains traits that we need to look at. Something else to be aware of is the psychopathic fiction: people with these sort of traits, sometimes create a world around themselves of fiction. You notice this in organisations sometimes - usually there's a bubble of people who think they're fantastic, and everyone else thinks that they're a real problem. Remember though, we're not looking at this in terms of clinical diagnosis. On a day to day level, not all traits are good - but we can look at the sort of behaviours that come up. I call these behaviours, *vampire behaviours.*

Vampires

For most of us the elephant isn't really that scary. It's not a Dark Triad elephant. That's just a bit of

13 By Cole Paviour

dramatization to get you to think about it. Sometimes a Dark Triad elephant does happen, but really not often. Most of the time, we're dealing with the kind of behaviours that can be changed. I wrote a book, on this very subject: *Changing Vampires into Angels - Six Steps to Heaven in Your Relationships*[58]. Because these behaviours can be changed. I have identified six different behavioural strategies that are prevalent in organisations, and in life. And they are unhealthy, and they are damaging, and we all need to be aware of them. Because we all might use them to some extent. And each one has got an antidote, which we will come to…

The cost of all this darkness

So, the Dark Triad, and more commonly, vampires, cause stress and illness, and they stop people from being able to perform. They lose you people. And you have to be aware of them. But how much do they actually cost you? How much does it cost you in not having managers and leaders who are affective and brainy, and able to engage? Ready? Here come the numbers!

---

[58] Paviour, M. (2002*). Changing Vampires into Angels - Six Steps to Heaven in your Relationships*. Isiliver Books.

EXAMPLE Industry statistics	No. days sickness absence per person pa	average salary pa	No. of employees	value of days lost to sickness pa	Savings on lost days
UK Average sick days	9.1	£25k	3000	£2.7m	
UK Engaged Company (Aspirational)	2.5	£25k	3000	£741k	£1.95m
Predicted sick days after intervention	6.1	£25k	3000	£1.8m	£889k

14 Costs of stress and illness to business

So, in the example we have an organisation with 3000 employees, earning on average £25k/year. If we look at sickness absence, just moving up a sensible amount - not to the most engaged, but moving up towards it - you could save £889,000 per year in lost days. And that is just sickness absence - there are lots of other things, and we're talking serious money here.

The return on investment of engagement

So, what difference does removing those barriers, and having emotionally engaged people actually make in terms of money?

• Double annual net profit

- 2.5 times revenue growth
- 35% increased efficiency
- 40% lower employee turnover
- 12% higher customer satisfaction
- 18% higher productivity

This is based on the government backed research carried out by McLeod and Clarke in 2011, for Engage for Success[59].

Now, not only have I written a book about this, I'm a psychologist - and I have also recently personally suffered at the hands of three different people, all of whom have maladaptive personality disorders, or issues; one of whom has a diagnosed disorder; it could happen to anyone! So you have to be aware of these behaviours. Hare has said that what tends to happen when you come across this sort of thing, is that it ends in either suicide, bankruptcy, or court cases. And that's very much what I can say I've come face to face with! It has a devastating effect. A client of mine has sold their business in order to get away from an individual who was a problem. And it wasn't a small business! And with another client – their staff attrition rate is terrible; everybody is leaving because the MD

---

[59] MacLeod and Clarke (2011) *Engaging for Success* [online] Available at
http://www.engageforsuccess.org/wp-content/uploads/2012/09/file52215.pdf

is a serious problem, with maladaptive personality issues. But the Board are saying "Well, he seems to know his numbers!" Hmm, yes! Another organisation, there's been a malpractising GP that the PCT turned their back on, because they didn't want to deal with the personality issue. This is serious stuff, and serious money, so that's why I'm passionate about doing something about it.

Angels - The Vampire Antidote

This is the angels of emotional engagement - they represent the antidote.

- Joy
- Acceptance
- Truth
- Courage
- Empowerment
- Passion

For me, they represent the six emotional qualities of A+B leadership. So let's consider each of these "angels" in detail.

Joy

How this manifests in work is vital to the emotional engagement of the team. As with all emotional behaviours we need to start with ourselves. This is leader behaviour not just team behaviour.

Richard Branson sees this as a vital part of his success, the importance of being able to laugh and have fun; that work should be its own reward.[60] This concept of intrinsic motivation is not new, but there are still those who believe that old Theory X style of leadership[61] - that people would avoid work if they could, and therefore that leaders should control contain. Where there is this kind of attitude there is transactional engagement at best. Naturally.

My personal philosophy is that I take my work very seriously, but I don't take myself too seriously. And that laughing a lot goes with working hard.

But there's more to joy that just fooling around a little, and its heavily linked to the other aspects. Having fun is a "Pleasant Life" form of happiness[62]. This is good, but not as enduring as the happiness of flow and service.

---

[60] Pink, D. (2011). *Drive*. Edinburgh: Canongate.

[61] McGregor, D. (1960). *The Human Side of Enterprise*, New York, McGrawHill. ISBN: 9780071462228

[62] Seligman, M. (2003). *Authentic happiness*. London: Nicholas Brealey.

Acceptance

I also call this aspect "love", but in a sense that is such a universal term it's difficult to get to grips with what that really means as a leader. So acceptance does the job.

Acceptance needs to be modelled and permitted. Vitally, this needs to relate to self-acceptance; that ability to be ok about yourself, no matter what.

When we show a lack of tolerance for our own shortcomings, we are actually modelling a lack of self-acceptance. Acceptance means saying its ok to make mistakes, because that is the way we grow and learn[63]. Tolerance for errors was something Tom Peters noted as an example of behaviours that created excellent organisations back in the 1980's. Although Tom accepts that not everything that he and Waterman identified in their In Search of Excellence books was as effective as they had believed, I think that without this kind of attitude you have no possibility of innovation and change. You will become a dinosaur.

---

[63] Richard *Branson - The Virgin Way: Everything I Know about Leadership ISBN: 9781591847373*

Truth

Everyone wants honesty, but do we live in a world of truth?[64] We all tell lies every single day – we are programmed to do so, from the small white lies to rather big old elephant shaped ones. Occasionally, one comes across someone who just tells it how it is, and many people find these folk rather uncomfortable!

How should we define honesty in terms of leadership and work?

"No one can lie to you without your approval. The liar and the recipient participate in a fabric of mythmaking together. A lie does not have power by its utterance – its power lies in someone agreeing to believe the lie" Pamela Meyer

Evidence shows that people are feeling less guilty about lying at work than in their personal lives.[65] So there is some gap here between our values at home and at work. And where there is that gap there will not be emotional engagement. It is in this

---

[64] Meyer, P. (2010). *Liespotting*. New York: St. Martin's Press.

[65] [65] Meyer, P. (2010). *Liespotting*. New York: St. Martin's Press.

scenario that your people will appear very engaged, but be completely disloyal if something better comes along. Or they may decide to take matters into their own hands – rewarding themselves a little too generously on those expenses again!

Learn the signs that your team are speaking honestly or dishonestly. Watch out for behaviours that include:

- Vocally: Being guarded or sidestepping the story. The words people say. If we are being honest we'll just talk about things, and not necessarily in chronological order. Liars will want to keep to a few basic statements, will smokescreen with whines about the interview and irrelevant details. And they will have a devil of a job telling the story out of sequence.

- Facially: Fake smiles or incongruent expressions – learn what each expression looks like[66] and then notice the facial expressions that dart into view for a moment or two. Remember that our brains are wired to our facial expressions. So if we are negotiating and I look contemptuous for a split second, then it probably means I'm feeling that way – so watch out!

---

[66] Ekman, P. (2004). *Emotions revealed*. London: Phoenix

- Body Language: Extraneous movements – especially around the mouth and face may be a giveaway that this person is being less than truthful. This is a childlike response as children cover their mouths when they lie. You would expect openness and body language should reflect this, open palms offered suggest "I'm receptive". Twisting away from you or closing the body off with tightly folded arms or pulling a book or bag in front of the body suggests hiding. And grasping the neck is a threat response – it may not mean lying, but it does mean that I'm feeling threatened – so be wary of assuming that a person feeling under threat is automatically a liar!

To create the honest and truthful environment that will reward you with performance and happiness you need to reward honesty at all costs. In other words, the truth, when spoken is sacrosanct. If we prize the truth over our

15 Unreceptive Badger by Tate

need to be "right" or to blame, and deal with reality positively, we have a recipe for success.[67]

---

[67] Richard *Branson - The Virgin Way: Everything I Know about Leadership ISBN: 9781591847373*

Courage

This one is very close to my heart. There are so few people who will have the courage to stand up and say when things are wrong. But some do. And, it may interest you to know that it is more likely to be a woman than a man at work. And black men (Afro-American Males in the study) who are eight times more likely to be "everyday heroes" than anyone else, having the courage to do a daring deed to save someone else's life.[68]

Courage is the over-riding quality of the much maligned whistle-blower. Standing firm for what you believe, refusing to allow wrong-doing to take place, no matter what happens to yourself; that's courage.

But courage happens on a daily basis, in small ways too. Having the courage to say: "I was wrong," when you may be ridiculed; "Help" when you may look incompetent; "I've got a new idea," when it may be "poo-pooed". This is all about courage.

As a leader we need to ensure that we engender our teams with this courage – by being prepared to be wrong and ridiculed, to look incompetent and to occasionally be "poo-pooed"!

---

[68] Zimbardo, P. (2009). *The Lucifer effect*. London: Rider.

Without acceptance and courage there is no vulnerability. And as Brene Brown says: without vulnerability there is no creativity, innovation and change.[69]

Empowerment

I sometimes call this Freedom. Here we are back to motivation. Autonomy is fundamental to motivation and also to empowerment. In order to ensure we have an atmosphere of empowerment we need to ensure people are given the opportunity to develop (mastery, as Dan Pink calls it).

The steps to empowerment are:

- Understanding that our mental processes can change.
- Freeing ourselves from threat response and anxiety
- Being enough[70]

We need to recognise that we are not perfect, but that is ok. We need to let our teams know that we accept them unconditionally.

---

[69] Brown, B TEDxHouston, (2010). *The Power of Vulnerability.* [video] Available at: http://www.ted.com/talks/brene_brown_on_vulnerability?language=en [Accessed 8 Sep. 2015].

[70] Brown, B. *The Gifts Of Imperfection.* Center City, Minn.: Hazelden, 2010. Print.

Passion

From purpose comes passion. When you believe in your mission, when it drives you to jump out of bed on a Monday morning shouting "hooray, more work!" then you know you have cracked this one.

Is it so very difficult? Actually, no. If we look we can find the real benefits and meaning in our work. And we need to share with our people the important role they have to play in making the world a better place.

When we work with our passion, and our bliss we discover a sense of wellbeing that overrides time and space.[71] We can even lose our pain and become healthier.[72] So it was never more important to find meaning and engage our passion than now. My approach has always been to fit the job to the person, to find what really makes their heart sing and then create a job around them. As a result I think I have amazingly motivated and incredibly passionate people in my team who always go the extra ten miles or so. They take the business personally. What could be better than that?

---

[71] Csikszentmihalyi, M. (2004). *Good Business: Leadership, Flow, and the Making of Meaning.* Penguin Books.

[72] Adams, P. (1998). *Gesundheit!.* Healing Arts Press.

Be a crazy person

I've learnt that there are angels in us all. But there are also vampires, and that we need to be prepared to shift that elephant, and not accept negative or maladaptive behaviours. We can't do this any longer - because we will be the ones who suffer in the end. I've learnt the need for courage, as well as understanding. And to be reasonably sceptical about people who look too good to be true - or who believe themselves to be beyond question. I've realised that when it feels wrong, it probably is wrong - even if the other person can talk their way out of it. I've learnt to trust my instincts, and not to feel I'm being negative when I notice negative things. That's difficult isn't it? Because we want to be positive. I've discovered very painfully, that it's not so good to be the little boy that shouts out the emperor hasn't got any clothes. There are better ways of doing this, and when you do shout it only makes you look mad. I've learnt that the elephant in the room can be shifted - sometimes by force. But more often, it can be shifted by listening, noticing, refusing to become complicit in lies and trusting ourselves, and sometimes trusting those people who may appear a little bit crazy. And I'm proud to consider myself one of those crazy people.

CHAPTER 4
A+B: Emotional Leadership

Why does Emotional Leadership matter? To understand why emotional awareness matters in work, we need to consider what is going on in the world of work today.

There has been a revolution in the way we do business, the technology revolution has changed many things about work. And one area that this had impacted upon strongly is motivation and morale.

This may not be an obvious connection, but we have recently discovered that people are just not motivated for the reasons we think. And more importantly, people cannot be forced to be motivated.

The businesses that are making all the headway and driving forward this revolution are often manned by people who don't even get paid! So if we are still thinking that money is the big motivator, well think again!

People work for people they like – and if they are going to be engaged and committed to their jobs, and their business, and their employer it is the manner by which they are lead that will make all the difference.

Whether you are a top manager or team supervisor, the results you get from your people are going to be dependent upon how you manage them. And how they feel about it.

As soon as I mention feelings I can sense people getting worried – "oh no, not group hugs!" I hear you saying, "Not sharing each other's experience and feelings in a supportive manner" I hear you cry, "Oh no, please, no tears and tissues!"

Well, fear not! The answer to all the above is a resounding no! So what I am going to do now is to explain why leading with the emotions is NOT about being touchy feely; how it REDUCES tears and tantrums; how it INCREASES high levels of professionalism; and how it creates commitment to your business.

And, most importantly, how it will make your department, team and organisation more successful and wealthier.

What are these emotions anyway?

There are some people who think that they do not feel emotions at work, and that they do not have an impact upon their decision making.

In a study by The Fortune Knowledge Group and gyro[73] top executives have identified that they make their decisions emotionally, and the one in the study who said he based his decisions on rationale, said that after applying logic his final decision was emotional!

This is not that surprising as the reality is that we are hardwired to feel emotions and base all our decision-making upon them. We look into this more in my course on Emotional Intelligence in Leadership. The key thing to remember right now, is that your inner experience is an emotional experience – and even if you like to live in your head, you still have an emotional inner life. And it also

---

http://www.gyro.com/igniting-now/news/new-study-emotion-trumps-data-for-business-decision-makers/

appears that if, for some reason, your ability to feel your emotions is damaged – your ability to make good quality decisions will be impaired.[74]

I work with many people who are not so sure about this. They tell me that they don't feel emotions at work. When I ask them, do you ever feel angry or frustrated? They answer, "Yes of course", so I think we should define, at this point what an emotion actually is!

Emotions are internal states of being a mental state.

The body can have reactions that may create an emotion – such as hearing an unusual sound and feeling afraid.

And we can have feelings that relate to emotions – such as feeling our stomachs "drop" on a rollercoaster and feeling excited and stimulated by it.

However, emotions have a deeper basis that just a feeling or a physiological (bodily process) reaction.

Although there is no clear understanding as to what comes first the thinking or the emotion, it is clear that we all experience emotions as part of every experience we have. So all the

---

[74] Bechara, A. (2000). Emotion, Decision Making and the Orbitofrontal Cortex. Cerebral Cortex, 10(3), pp.295-307. [Online] Available at:http://tamar.tau.ac.il/Genome2Brain2008/Human%20Brain/Damasio%20Emotions%20and%20Decision%20Making.pdf (accessed 2 September 2015)

people who say they don't have emotions at work may have simply not noticed what they have been experiencing.

This is important.

Until we can understand our own responses to situations, and the vitalness of our emotions on everything we say and do, we cannot begin to understand how we can effectively work with others, run our teams, create loyal customers and develop a business that is profitable; because all business requires people – whether they be customers, clients, employees, contractors or leaders.

What is Affectiveness?

The basic premise behind the concept of Affective Brainy Leadership is this:

Everything I do has an emotional affect on you; and everything you do has an emotional affect upon me"

As the evidence proves emotions are experienced by us all, all of the time, and they motivate our behaviour. So affective goes towards the brain from what we sense, and effective is what action we take via the motor neurons from our brain. Like seeing a glass of water and fancying a drink (affective) and then grabbing it and taking a swig (effective).

We can alter our own emotions, and, indeed we can use facial behaviours to create significant changes in our mental state. It is also possible that we can influence the mental / emotional state of others through our behaviours. This can be seen in animal behaviour – such as an aggressive dog which would be ears, tail, hair, and back up and a submissive dog doing the opposite – ears, tail, hair and back down; or primates which indicate aggression with eye contact and submission with avoiding eye contact.

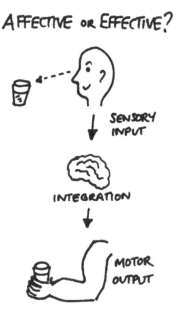

16 Affective or Effective? © Maria Paviour Company Ltd 2015

What about in your life – have you noticed how people can use aggressive behaviours and invoke submissive in others – or create a stand-off.

We can also influence with positive emotions such as laughing and causing others to smile or laugh.

It begins to become obvious that we all impact upon each other emotionally, and furthermore, this is all part of a survival mechanism, that has become extremely sophisticated in humans.

Our expressions and emotions are manifold, and our reactions to the expression of emotions in others are complex, but actually can be analysed and understood when we have the right vocabulary for this (see my course on The Emotional Vocabulary for more details).

As our lives are centred on the processes that are going on in our minds, we need to realise that emotions are actually also going on in our minds – and that the physical sensations we have that accompany them may be only labels we apply or symptomatic of the emotion itself.

We also must realise that emotions are a vital component of our programming, and if we do not respond to them in ourselves and others we are failing to provide a complete response. In fact, what actually happens is we choose to believe that our emotions are unimportant compared to our logic, as a way of avoiding dealing with the complexity of human relationships.

This is not the same as not having emotions – it is "pretending" we don't have emotions. And sometimes we do such a good job at this we numb down the feelings so that we believe that we are being reasonable and rational. The only trouble is, our teams, customers and employees may not have the same experience.

So every time I determine that my emotions are not important, I am failing to recognise that my demeanour is portraying an emotion that is affecting someone else – because they are programmed to receive that information.

To become truly great leaders we need to be capable of sending and adapting messages so that they create the reactions and responses that we want and that will support our success.

Only those who can develop this level of Emotional Intelligence will become great leaders. They may become highly paid senior people – but they won't be great leaders.

Organisation and Efficiency

A very basic level skill required for a leader is the ability to organise - or at the very least know what should be done to organise.

Organisation can lead to efficiency. Efficiency is whereby you can create more in quantity for the same investment in time/energy/resources. An efficient manager may produce vast quantities of paperwork very quickly. The quality of this paperwork and how beneficial it is remains to be questioned - perhaps it is required, perhaps not - but the efficiency is in being able to produce the work rapidly.

All leaders need to understand this, and there are times when working hard and getting things done is just what is required. However, there are times when you need to stand back and ask those questions like - why are we doing this? Is it of benefit to us? How?

When you start asking these sorts of questions you are moving round the triangle to "management" and effectiveness.

Management - a Matter of Strategy and Tactics

We often hear people complaining about a lack of strategy! But what is strategy, exactly?

In simple terms, the word derived from the military and the plan of action to be applied in order to win in battle. So we could think of our strategy as our way of planning to win in business.

However, within the overall strategy, there are the tactics. So what are these? Well the tactics are the means of achieving the strategic plan. So our strategy might be to get a large market share very quickly, and our tactics might be to advertise strongly and sell cheaply in order to achieve this.

Why does this matter, is it just all words - just semantics? Well, yes, and no! In the end it's what happens in the end that counts and not what you call it - but the thing is you need to remember that strategy without tactics is a plan without a way forward to achieve it; and tactics without a strategy is a lot of activity going nowhere fast!

So yes, you do need both; and you need to think about how these can move you to better effectiveness.

Being effective means getting more result for your pound/time/effort. Please notice the word "result". It is not a matter of just getting more done, it's a matter of getting better results. So sometimes it is not efficient, but can be effective. A good example is in taking lots of time to secure a new customer. It may not be efficient use of your time, but it is effective if it wins you the deal.

The role of A+B Leadership

How does the idea of A+B Leadership fit into the way in which we work in organisations today, and how we achieve our aspirations and goals?

At the most basic level we need to be capable of organising. This is the first edge, as this is where we can create some efficiency in business practice – however, efficiency is simply doing the same thing as quickly as possible, and this in itself is not sufficient for business success.[75].

Management enables us to move from mere efficiency to effectiveness[76] – this is where Professor Bill Reddin comes in – now he is fundamentally important to my ideal of A+B leadership. And I don't know why he is not as well-known as so many others. Blanchards' situational leadership model[77] is all very lovely, and I do use it, but Reddin really did get the idea when he built in the importance of how well we relate to

---

[75] Adair, J. (1973) *Action Centred Leadership*, US: McGraw-Hill Inc

[76] Reddin, W. (1987). How to make your management style more effective. London: McGraw-Hill.

[77] Hersey, P. and Blanchard, K. H. (1977). *Management of Organizational Behavior: Utilizing Human Resources* (3rd ed.) New Jersey: Prentice Hall

others. Here are the two models, I really do think that you need both!

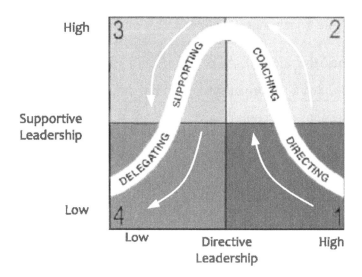

17 After Hershey and Blanchard, Situational Leadership

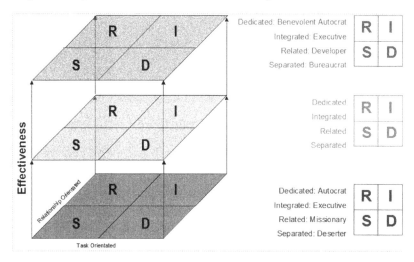

18.After Reddin

To make the most of this you need to refer to the learning curve model. I review this in a bit more detail later on. But right now the key is in recognising the process of learning. We start off not knowing what we don't know – we are unaware of what is required from us, and so we may even think that the task we are about to learn looks easy, because the person doing it makes it look easy. We are, at this point an Unconscious Incompetent – we don't know what we don't know. Stage two we learn and become aware of how much there is to learn. We are conscious incompetents – we know what we don't know, but we can feel dejected by how very much there is to learn. There is surely nothing worse in learning a new skill than becoming aware of how incompetent you are. At this point we've really moved a long way along the learning curve; but it just feels like we're going backwards.

After a while we learn the skill and we can do it when we think about it – so now we are consciously competent. I may not feel very confident though, it's difficult to believe that I've actually got it, but I have. I need lots of boosting and a little gentle letting go of the hand so I can go it alone.

Finally, I'll get my confidence and I'll be performing as an Unconscious Competent. Now I just need to be pointed in the right direction and I'm off. If you review the Blanchard model you will see how it complements each stage. When I'm new in the task I get lots of directions and instructions, as I get to the crisis of conscious incompetence I need to receive loads of coaching and support. Then this eases off a little as I need to grow my confidence by trying for myself as a Conscious Competent. And finally, off I go, just delegate me the task I know I'm up to it.

Reddin's model shows that situational leadership can be both effective and ineffective. I would argue that being ineffective is also being inaffective (if that's a word). It's clear that Reddin developed his model around emotional competencies, not just functional ones. After all it is ok to say I'll direct you today, but there is good and bad directing.

A+B leadership is the third edge of the triangle. This is where you move from those two important elements of efficiency and effectiveness and get to the nub of the issue – commitment or emotional engagement.

19 *The Affective Leadership Triangle, Maria Paviour*

All three sides of the triangle are essential to achievement in business. Successful leaders often have the qualities of affectiveness naturally, and therefore achieve commitment from their staff that elevates their success. Some leaders become successful through tyranny – but the people will not stay with a tyrannical boss if they have a choice. And those who do stay may believe they aren't capable of anything else, as they have lost their self-confidence.

Building self-belief, self-empowerment and self-confidence will improve your business – it is common sense.

In order to become great, you must progress through the process of becoming acceptable, then good. And in turn this means being good at organisation, understanding strategy and tactics, and ultimately leading the way forward.

To summarize: A+B Leadership is based on the premise "everything I do has an emotional affect on you and everything you do has an emotional affect on me"

A+B Leadership is the base line of the triangle of leadership: Organising (efficiency) managing (effectiveness) and leading (commitment) because this is where we get emotional engagement from our people.

PART 2
Getting Emotionally Engaged

"I would like to say I enjoyed this first day at school.

I realize the teachers have put in a lot of effort, and a host of administrators have worked hard to develop our current scholastic program. The PTA has also done its share as have the school custodians.

Therefore, I would like very much to say I enjoyed this first day at school.

But I didn't!"

Sally Brown (Charlie Brown's sister)[78]

---

[78] Charles Schulz – Peanuts http://www.gocomics.com/peanuts/1963/09/09/

CHAPTER 5

What makes us work?

W ell, we need to want to work, or we will do the bare minimum, and it is universally accepted that having staff that do more than the bare minimum is a good thing!

If we are prepared to go the extra mile it's because we feel a sense of commitment to our employer. I look into this in more detail in the part on motivation, but for now, let's just think about engagement.[79]

[79] MacLeod and Clarke (2011) *Engaging for Success* [online] Available at
http://www.engageforsuccess.org/wp-content/uploads/2012/09/file52215.pdf

Recent research from the CIPD [80] demonstrates that there are two types of engagement:

Transactional engagement – whereby we are engaged in the task. For example, we may love the job we do, or the profession we are in – but this doesn't mean we are committed to our company.

Emotional engagement – whereby we are emotionally committed to the company/team as well as the job.

If you have a team of people who are transactionally engaged they may want to stay in the same profession, but they may not care who they work for.

If you have a team who are emotionally engaged or committed they work for you for the love of the organisation.

---

[80] CIPD (May 2012) *CIPD: Emotional or transactional engagement – does it matter?* Kingston Engagement Consortium 23.05.12

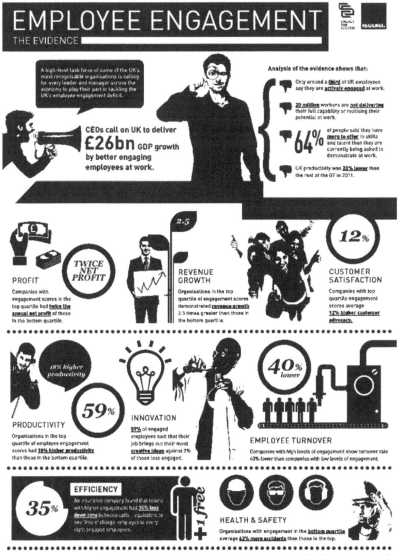

20 The Engage for Success Infographic, available at www.engageforsuccess.org

Companies and organisations that inspire this level of engagement are usually well known for having staff who love their jobs, and a queue of people who want to work for them. If you haven't worked it out already, emotionally engaged people are what you need to be striving for.

And emotional commitment requires A+B leadership. The leadership comes first, the commitment comes second.

Trust – the people in the business need to trust the organisation and their boss.

Trust is a fundamental pre-requisite to employee commitment, and it is made up of a combination of emotional factors. It has been shown that the emotions affect the way people make decisions, even complex ones, and this includes whether to trust someone or not.

A 2011 study[81] discovered that trust was significantly reduced by negative emotions, most especially when they felt little control over their circumstances.

The emotion that caused the greatest impact upon trust was anxiety, as this emotion relates to a difficulty in predicting

---

[81] Myers, D., & Tingley, D. (Working Paper 2011) *The Influence of Emotion on Trust* [online] Available at: http://scholar.harvard.edu/files/dtingley/files/emotionmanipulationm11.pdf

outcomes. We usually become fearful or anxious when we don't know the result or have little control over it.

Trust is a vital component of commitment within a business. If your employees don't trust the business they will not remain.

Current research has shown a very low level of trust in senior leaders of organisations, and so this issue is of great significance today.

The CIPD found that only 36 per cent of workers trust their top leaders, while 58 per cent of employees display signs of a 'not bothered' attitude to their job, according their report, *Employee Outlook Summer 2012* .[82]

The study found that people who trusted their leaders didn't appear to suffer as much stress.

It also found that 58 per cent of staff with a 'neutral engagement' level were also half as likely to 'go the extra mile' compared to those who were positively engaged, and nearly three times more likely to be looking for a new job. This is not good news for a business who wants employees to be committed.

---

[82] CIPD (2012) *Employee Outlook Summer 2012* [online] available at:
http://www.cipd.co.uk/binaries/employee-outlook_2012-summer.pdf

Peter Cheese, CEO of the CIPD said [83]

"Given the number of examples reported in the media in recent months of unethical behaviours and corrosive cultures overseen by senior leaders, it is perhaps unsurprising to see trust in the workplace eroding,"

"What's worrying is the impact this will have on engagement. We know that strong employee engagement drives higher productivity and better business outcomes, so such a prominent display of 'neutral engagement' in the workplace should act as a real wake up call for employers."

In order to develop affectiveness, create engagement and promote a successful business we need to take action in terms of the way we impact upon others.

To be fit to lead we need to be "hardy", not the sort of toughness that we may have been led to imagine that leaders should have – a brutally, bottom-line driven and hard hearted attitude, no, the new leaders need to be committed to life as

---

[83] CIPD (2012) 'Article' People Management, July 2012, Corporate scandals 'damaging employee engagement' By John Eccleston on 23 Jul 2012

well as work, curious and attentive; we need to have some belief that we can influence things and enjoy the challenge of change.[84]

Qualities of Transactional Engagement

What does it mean to be engaged in your work? Firstly, let's consider being transactionally engaged.

Transactional engagement is usually identified in engagement surveys – but they may not identify emotional engagement. The problem with transactional engagement is that people may not tell you the whole truth as they are not fully emotionally involved with the business.

A transactionally engaged employee will put their self-interest before the business, but this doesn't mean they do not do a good job. They may be very involved in the task itself, and the joy and satisfaction of a job well done may provide ample motivation for them to do very well.

What you will not see is an employee who cares about the business and who wants to remain with the business. They will not share the values, or if they do, they will not recognise the

---

[84] Susan Kobasa's "hardiness" provided a framework for characteristics whereby behaviours/dispositions that managers who worked in stressful environments did not suffer the ill effects of stress employed

business values (in other words, they don't believe them or believe in them).[85]

In an engagement survey, a transactionally engaged person may answer the questions the way they think the employee wants them to. They say what they think you want to hear.

Qualities of Emotional Engagement

An emotionally engaged employee will work for you because they love the company.

This seems to be at odds with the harsh world of commerce, but it's true. People want to be a part of something they love, and the more experienced and talented they are the more true this becomes.

But the important thing in this overview of A+B Leadership is to understand that many people put their emotional commitment before pay or benefits.

If you have employees who are emotionally committed they are more likely to go the extra mile in terms of their work and hours, they are less likely to complain about stress, and feel better in themselves. They are likely to share their experiences of working for you positively with friends, family and

---

[85] CIPD (May 2012) *CIPD: Emotional or transactional engagement – does it matter?* Kingston Engagement Consortium 23.05.12

acquaintances, and they will show exceptional levels of loyalty.

Consequently the results you get from an emotionally committed team surpass any others. Think about some businesses that have clearly emotionally engaged staff: The Body Shop was a good example, particularly when run by Anita Roddick[86]; Virgin[87]; Bannatyne's Health Clubs[88] are all examples; you probably know others.

Emotionally engaged people want to be part of something they love. They go the 'extra mile'

21 Tortoise to come out of shell By Jazz

Emotional commitment requires A+B leadership. The leadership comes first, the commitment comes second.

Trust is the key component in 'creating followership'. When trust is present, people will commit, and emotionally engage with us and the organisation.

---

[86] Roddick, A. (1991). *Body and soul*. New York: Crown.

[87] Schawbel, D. (2015). *Richard Branson's Three Most Important Leadership Principles.* [online] Forbes. Available at: http://www.forbes.com/sites/danschawbel/2014/09/23/richard-branson-his-3-most-important-leadership-principles/ [Accessed 15 Sep. 2015].

[88] Bannatyne, D. (2011). *43 Mistakes Businesses Make--And How To Avoid Them.* London: Headline Pub.

"Brainy" Neuroscience for Engaged People

CHAPTER 6
What makes an A+B leader?

THE FOUR QUADRANTS OF A+B LEADERSHIP

	External - Environmental	Internal - Personal
	Organisational Forward Pathway	Individualised Forward Pathway
FUTURE	Results in sense of: ACHIEVEMENT	Demonstrated by: HAPPINESS
	Emotional Structure	Emotional Behaviour
CURRENT	Results in sense of: SECURITY	Demonstration by: SELF-EXPRESSION

22 Factors Driving Emotional Commitment at Work, Copyright Maria Paviour 2012

In order to become an A+B Leader you need to be aware of the Four Quadrants of A+B Leadership.

The Four Quadrants

In order to create a sense of emotional commitment in your team and organisation you need to ensure that you have considered the following:

1. The environment and how it affects performance.

2. The Individual and their needs

3. The organisation and its aims and aspirations

When these aspects are in place you can then move towards

4. The happiness and well-being of the organisation and everyone in it.

Happiness is not just a nice idea, it is essential for the highest level of performance. It is proven through the latest psychological research, that when the right pieces of the jigsaw are in place employees can perform at such a high level they create a "flow" that means that they can process information faster than would usually be consciously possible.

When this happens they perform at their best, produce outstanding work and feel a deep sense of happiness which is known as "flow".

As you can see each of these four aspects noted above are contained within the A+B Leadership Grid.

The Physical Environment

The way we respond to work, and how committed we feel is dependent upon the environment we exist within. I look at this in terms of the emotional environment and the physical environment.

Physical environment – this relates to the place within which we work. Obviously, there are health and safety attributes that must be taken into account in order to make the workplace suitable, but beyond that there are also the feelings that the environment evokes in the individual.

A messy environment isn't just unsightly, it is also difficult to find the right information at the right time; working in this kind of space makes you feel more stressed as a result.

If you study Feng Shui, the Chinese Art of Placement, you will see that most of it is applied common sense. For example, sitting with your back to a door is considered poor positioning

– but the practical side of this is that sitting in this position creates a sense of mild anxiety as you cannot see if someone is approaching you or entering the room.

Making the sure the physical environment is fit for purpose, and that it also lifts the spirits is a simple and yet important element of creating the right environment for A+B Leadership. However, it is not enough on its own! There was never a company that achieved emotional commitment from its staff because it decorated the office! But you can help depress commitment if you don't.

The emotional environment

This aspect is of overwhelming significance. The emotional environment varies in an organisation according to the people who inhabit the environment.

Emotional Environment – the atmosphere and/or the norms and values that are palpably present in the environment through the manner in which people communicate with each other[89].

---

[89] Newton J and Davis J (2014) 'Three Secrets of Organisational Effectiveness' *Strategy+Business* 14 July [Online] available at: http://www.strategy-business.com/article/00271?gko=d819d (accessed 2 September 2015)

The way in which we structure our emotional environment either creates security or insecurity with our people. And ourselves.

If you think about the emotional environment you exist within at the moment, you can probably identify those aspects that create a sense of security and those that undermine it.

Feeling secure is an emotional response. We put together a whole lot of different experiences and then label the physical sensations that they cause in our bodies. For some people security may be an absence of feelings of anxiety; or it may be a sense of relaxation. Both of these need to be connected to a cognitive thought process that reviews other elements in the environment.

For example: I like working with John and Betty, they demonstrate support for me by being kind and helpful, and I also feel relaxed because we can laugh together and often do. I always feel I can ask for help or say what I think or feel. This gives me a sense of physical relaxation, I feel grounded and light in spirit.

The above is an example of cognitive processes that lead to a feeling and that is termed an emotion. Notice terms such as light in spirit. When you drill down into a term like that you can often find the physical reactions that relates to it. In this case, it could relate to a sense of feeling well oxygenated – because breathing is effective rather than laboured or rapid.

Emotional Behaviour and Self Expression - All behaviour is emotional

I would argue that all behaviour is emotional – in that it is almost impossible to behave completely dispassionately about anything. We can, of course, be aware of our emotions and cognitively calculate risks or potential outcomes, but our emotions are usually responsible for any final decisions we make.

If you think about the biggest purchase you will ever make – buying a house – then you may find a property that "ticks all the boxes" but your final decision will be based upon "if you like it". You will make your ultimate decision based on emotions.

Emotions help us to survive

Let's be clear, emotions are not a bad thing! They are part of our sophisticated survival strategy, and, indeed when we listen to our "inner voice" or respond to our "gut instinct" all we are doing is responding to the emotional centres messages –

23 Quacking Up
by Jazz

remember: this part of the brain does not deal in language, which is why we may find it difficult to put into words *why* we want to make the decision that we want to make – but the unconscious part of our brain just knows.

The second quadrant of A+B Leadership

The second quadrant of A+B Leadership relates to how individuals respond to their emotional environment. This can be a bit of a chicken and egg situation. The emotional environment can be created by the way people respond – so that their behaviour within the environment creates the environment. However, the important element here is that in being clear about what the environment needs to be, we can then monitor the behaviours within it.

Constant adjustment

It is not possible to create a perfect environment and then have everyone all happily dancing to work full of joy and compassion every day! That would be great, but it's not realistic. The fact is, that even with a well thought through emotional environment people will still have their own emotions and reactions. So a vital part of A+B Leadership is the constant monitoring to keep on course. It's a bit like steering a ship – you can easily over-steer and therefore overcompensate, and sometimes it takes a while for your adjustments in direction to come into effect.

The Forward Pathway

As well as having the environment right, and monitoring the way in which people express themselves so that we can make the relevant adaptions, we need to be thinking about the future.

Setting the future in the present

A+B Leadership requires us to be clear about how we set the tone for our team fulfilling the organisation's forward pathway. In a way this is like creating a picture of what the environment will be in the future – it's telling the story and engaging people in the purpose of the business.

When we are clear on our future path we can see how and when we are achieving. A sense of being a part of something that is making a difference is vital to high levels of engagement and commitment.

24 Supermouse by Jazz

Happiness creates stellar performance

When our team feel that sense of achievement – know what they need to do and can do it, they will respond to that with a sense of satisfaction. The ultimate goal is to create an environment in which the ability to work towards the organisation's future goals in terms of skills is dovetailed with the sense of challenge. When this is perfectly balanced your team will feel at their happiest at work. And, their performance will be stellar.[90]

To summarise, to become an A+B Leader you must be aware of the Four Quadrants of A+B Leadership.

1. The environment and how it affects performance.

2. The individual and their needs

3. The organisation and its aims and aspirations

When these aspects are in place you can then move towards:

4. The happiness and well-being of the organisation and everyone in it.

---

[90] Achor, S. (2011). *The happiness advantage*. London: Virgin.

CHAPTER 7
Putting the Foundations in Place

FACILITATING EMOTIONAL COMMITMENT

	Active	Responsive
	Leader Behaviour: CREATE	Leader Behaviour: ORIENTATE
FUTURE	Projective -Conceiving, imagining, stating Motive -Mission, drivers, purpose	Perspective -Time, sense, beliefs Adaptive -Challenge, mastery, balance
	Leader Behaviour: MODEL	Leader Behaviour: ANALYSE
CURRENT	Emotive -ergonomics, emotional vocabulary, values Interactive -"O.k.ness" Mindfulness, Empathy	Cognitive -"As if", Worst Case, Testing Interrogative -Experience Questions, assumptions questions, beliefs questions

25 Affective Leadership to Facilitate Emotional Commitment, copyright Maria Paviour 2012

As you can see from the grid above, taking the basic concepts of A+B leadership and turning them into reality requires you to develop key skills.

The 4 Key A+B Leadership Behaviours

An A+B leader should be carrying out four different behaviours on a day to day basis.

The leader should:

Analyse - the responses of their team in order to determine how they are relating to the environment.

Model - the behaviours that are most conducive to high levels of performance and commitment

Create - the forward pathway of the organisation in terms of building a picture and sense of what it will look and sound like, what it means and how it shall be.

Orientate - the individuals through the way in which work is structured in line with individual skills and needs.

Being Non Emotional Creates More Emotions

Why does a non-emotional approach create more emotional outbursts?

It's quite simple. A+B Leadership manages emotions. Non A+B Leadership creates them.

What do I mean by that? Well, if you have worked for an employer who doesn't show an emotional response to you, it creates a number of reactions:

- Attention seeking
- Cheating or One-Upmanship
- Apathy
- Sabotage

This may seem extreme, but, if you have no response from someone, you will ensure you get some response.

Attention seeking behaviours may include:

- over-reacting to small issues
- overly forceful characters – providing a charisma overload
- making a joke of everything even when things are serious - making a joke can be a great diffuser; it becomes attention seeking when it's inappropriate such as lampooning other team members -or the boss- cruelly.

Cheating or One-upmanship behaviours may include:

- Trying to "get one over" on the boss of the business – fiddling expenses, not completing a report, telling lies about who did what or whether work was done to deadline or regarding communications with clients.

- Playing the semantics game "I didn't actually say I did xyz, what I said was…"
- Manoeuvring one's position to show one's self in a better light than a team mate.
- Making snide comments about a team mates work to diminish their reputation

Apathetic behaviours may include:

- Moaning, but not taking action
- Being perpetually tired
- Looking and acting bored
- Lack or energy or interest

Sabotage behaviours may include;

- Undermining new schemes
- Setting up reasons for failure before beginning, and then creating a self-fulfilling prophecy
- Refusing to follow procedure or protocol
- Complaining to customers or other external people about the business or the team

It's quite plain that failing to respond to emotions can create serious difficulties for leaders.

Modelling the Emotive

The emotive element of the environment is the aspect that causes an emotional reaction, although it may not be directly related to communication or relationships. You need to ensure that the way you manage your personal space, as well as the group space, reflects the way in which you want people to respond, and in such a way that it promotes security among the team.

For example, if you want to create an emotional environment that is calm, organised and effective you will not promote this if the environment is messy, filing is left out with wobbly skyscraper piles of paperwork on desks, surfaces covered with objects that haven't been put away and out of date noticeboards.

In addition, you need to have an understanding of the emotional vocabulary so that you can interpret reactions. By understanding how to talk about emotions, the leader models to the team how they too can communicate their emotions; and, indeed, how they should not.

Most importantly, the leader needs to embody their values in their behaviours. These can be business values alone, or the personal values of the leader. I advocate both. If you do not engage with the organisation's values at a personal level then you are certainly not emotionally engaged.

Modelling Interactive Skills

Communication happens all the time

Communication is the most powerful way to create an environment. We are all communicating all the time, through our body posture, facial expressions as well as what we say.

And the words we speak are only a small part of the overall message, as tone of voice is of great significance when trying to interpret meaning.

Covert Communication

Not all communication is designed to directly convey a message to another person. Much of our communication is covertly aimed at communicating our mood, whether we want to be disturbed, whether we want to be rescued, whether we disapprove or feel apathetic and so on.

Interactions

The manner in which we interact with people is also a collection of different messages, and not all of them match. Sometimes we can say one thing with our words and yet mean something completely different. As a leader we need to be sending congruent messages – in other words, all the communication must match. We need to say what we mean. In order to do this we need to start from a position of feeling OK in ourselves and OK about others.

Being "OK"

We look into OKness in detail in the course "Understanding Ourselves", but at this point it is important to appreciate that feeling OK about who we are, and self-acceptance, are vital pre-requisites to A+B Leadership.[91]

The A+B Leadership programme is really more about how we related to ourselves first and others second, because unless you have dealt with your own demons, the things that make you react in the way that you do, and that create the "life script" that you create for yourself, you will be unable to deal with issues effectively in others.

---

[91] Harris, T (1995) *I'm OK, You're OK* Arrow, New Ed Edition ISBN 9780099552413

Being OK extends to our view of other people too. We need to accept others for who they are, no matter what they do. When we can separate actions from the person we can communicate in a way that creates security and commitment.

Mindfulness

Being mindful, being aware of yourself and noticing your own reactions, is another vital pre-requisite. When we apply mindfulness, we are noticing in the present moment the emotions and responses we are feeing, and are able to acknowledge them, and respond appropriately and effectively. In being mindful we become A+B, as we are aware of our emotions and therefore how they may affect others.

Empathy

Empathy, the ability to understand what it feels like to be another person, is the third vital pre-requisite to A+B leadership. Until you have appreciated that we all have emotions, empathy is redundant, because it is the act of understanding how someone feels, rather than just what they think.

Ideas can be expressed in words, on the page or through speech, but empathy requires that we read the emotions that are attached to those words.

Analysis – Responding to Individual Needs

One of the things about the A+B Leadership Model is that it isn't going to work! I know it sounds crazy to say it, but it's true, because no model that involves living and breathing human beings will work – for the very reason that human beings are not machines, and will insist on being human!

I admit this early on, because this model of leadership has built-in a feedback loop so that you can continually monitor and adjust your leadership behaviours, and consequently facilitate the engagement of your employees. When employees are engaged you are less likely to experience "psychological game playing".

Psychological games people play at work

The are many varieties of these games which originate from behaviours that I describe as "vampiristic" in that they create an energy drain on the team.

By energy drain, I refer to the time, resources and effort that people put into these individuals when they are using these vampiristic behaviours.

The games usually centre on the need to be accepted, whilst not believing oneself to be good enough.[92]

Where do these games come from? The best way of explaining this is the concept of a "schema" (more on this later) but in simple terms, we create a little internal programme that is constantly running in the background. Essentially, a group of neurons have become wired together by continual use.

I explain to my NeuroChemical Coaching™ clients that these are neurons wired to run these thought patterns. The brain is plastic and can change. The programme is not the person – it is just a piece of programme.

This is important, because we can lose ourselves in these pieces of programming. They are often small cyclical thinking patterns – and they are not who we are.

Why do we have these programmes?

The answer is – survival. We learn, from very young how to survive, and we wire that in. That may sound counter-intuitive – you may well ask: "why would I create a negative bit of thinking, a negative belief, just to help me survive – it's horrible and makes me feel bad". Yes, but it also limits your

---

[92] Berne E (2010) *Games People Play - the psychology of human relationships* Penguin ISBN 0141040270

behaviours, it keeps you away from things that may be a threat.

Remember this is the new social ecology – we aren't fighting sabre tooth tigers (if we ever did, must check my evolutionary history) – we are surviving in a social world. We are using basic survival mechanisms in a world that has changed faster than we can evolve. Mind you, I'm the queen of vintage and I rather like this old-fashioned brain of ours – it has a certain charm.

Breaking your programming

To break the programme we need to understand the programme.

Maybe an example will help at this point.

Let's say, I have a piece of programming that says I have no friends and that no one really likes me. This little programme is running in the background. Why? Because it has become a survival mechanism. For some reason, in my past, it became safer for me to avoid making friends, perhaps because of the pain of rejection. The problem is, this becomes a "script", this is what we call a small piece of programming that is entrenched. And once we have added up two and two and made "script" (regardless of the truth) we act in every way possible to "prove" that script.

We create situations in which we can then say – look, I was right.

Take my example. I believe no one likes me, so I avoid seeing people. There it is, proof. I never go out because I have no friends – as no one likes me.

Let's say I go to the pub. There's no one there – apart from Mathilda and her pet cricket. Mathilda is all right, but the pet cricket gets right on my nerves. So, here I am proving that no one likes me, because there is no one for me to talk to at the Pub.

Wait a minute, let's play that again. Actually, I believe that I make friends easily. When I go to the pub I notice there is someone there, how lovely, its Mathilda! And she has that pet cricket with her again. Now, to be honest I'm not keen on the cricket, but I've heard that they can be a good luck charm. And even if that cricket has to keep bringing the conversation round to whose playing at The Oval, or The Ashes or something, well, it's only because he's an enthusiast with limited life experience. So maybe he's not so bad after all. I'll go over and say hello.

You may have noticed that the second example was breaking the programming. When we notice a limiting belief, we need to "reframe" the situation. One method is to get into a "metaposition" that is, to stand outside yourself for a moment. My favourite way is to ask my clients to imagine a friend in the same situation as they have described about themselves. What advice would they give their friend? Amazing how easy it is to do this for a friend and not for oneself: "Don't be silly, of course people like you, and the cricket is just obsessed with his own interests, it's nothing personal".

Thinking is the problem

It seems so easy, doesn't it, to say – it's just a piece of programming. Why is it so difficult to alter this?

Well the problem is the thinking. Thinking your way out of thinking is horribly difficult. Don't think about an elephant…there we are, you're thinking about one, aren't you.

Telling someone to stop thinking something is impossible. But do not despair. First notice the schema at work, and then identify what survival mechanism is running it. As a leader, your job is to remove the threat from the situation, and coach the team member into a new schema.

Dealing with Games

When "psychological games" arise, think about the background survival programme that may be running before you challenge them.

In other words, it helps to have an idea about what may be behind the behaviour – and if we remember that it is a survival mechanism it removes the emotional elements allowing us to develop A+B solutions. Affective and Brainy solutions include knowing what drives the behaviour (A) and then developing a structure for altering the behaviour (B).

The 'A's' of Psychological Games

"It's all too much"

The employee has an angry outburst and then bursts into tears saying they are under terrible stress.

By bursting into tears, we may protect ourselves from others attacking us for our anger. An outburst of anger, is often due to pent up feelings. We don't feel safe to say how we really feel.

"I'm leaving"

The employee threatens to leave the business if their demands are not met.

It may be intended to force a change, it is not necessarily a real threat.

Leader's role is to make calm discussion of emotions and concerns ok.

Sarcasm or Inappropriate Joking

Team member is directly or subtly sarcastic with you or other team members, or makes a joke at your expense in front of the team which they believe demonstrates that they know something you don't.

The team member is playing one-upmanship.

Leader's role is to set boundaries for behaviours with the team that apply to everyone, including oneself. Would this joke be ok if the leader made it about a team member? If not, then it's not ok.

"Yes, but...."

Employee complains to you about a problem, but every solution you offer they reply with "yes, but..."

The employee want to prove their script that nothing will work.

Leader's role is to hand over the solution to the employee and to stop trying to "rescue" him or her.

"We all think"

The employee takes on the role of self-nominated spokesperson, and thinks they can speak about injustices to others, regardless of whether the others want them to or not.

Leader's role is to test the validity of the spokespersons comments rather than to take them as read.

"That customer is a complete swine!"

The team member blames and catastrophizes about a customer, refusing to accept any responsibility for the situation.

The team member may be taking something personally, to reinforce a script about how people treat them.

Leader's role is to ensure the team member feels accepted first, and then they can calmly review the situation objectively. In other words, when a team member blames it is only a discharge of discomfort and pain (Brene Brown).

"I can't"

The employee doubts their ability to perform and refuses to accept that they have the competence or that they can change their attitude to the situation.

The employee is in a helpless state which ensures they can avoid failure.

Leader's role is to provide opportunities for small wins, and then reinforce these with praise and acceptance.

"It always ends up being me!"

The team martyr and will do everything, whilst ensuring that they attract a lot of attention in the process. When offered help, they refuse in a martyr-like fashion.

They do not believe it is safe to ask for help, they do not believe that they deserve it.

Leader's role is to ensure the team members feels accepted and to tackle the underlying issue head on.

Team Clown/ Team Know-it-all

In both cases the employee demands attention.

They gain acceptance from these behaviours, they feel afraid, insecure or slighted about people in authority, they may believe that they deserve more and that things are "unfair".

Leader's role is to use these behaviours positively – the team clown can help lighten the mood when needed and the know-it-all can be supportive of new people or deal with problems.

"Don't upset him/her…"

The employee who has a reputation for being difficult, so that the team have to "step on egg shells" around them.

The employee uses a bad mood and possible outbursts to control the environment and everyone in it. It would suggest that they do not feel accepted or valuable in their own right.

Leader's role is to clarify what behaviours are and are not acceptable, and to monitor the emotional environment. The leader needs to be courageous in tackling a negative atmosphere.

These are a few examples, there are many more you can probably think of yourself from your own experience.

The 'B's' of Psychological Games

This is the Brainy bit. Here are some of the tactics you could employ to deal with these games.

Interrogative - Asking questions

Help the employee to recognise the glitches in their own reasoning and thinking, and encourage them to challenge their perceptions so that they can view things from a different angle, get a new perspective and review the way they hear the messages.

There are three questioning types that are most effective:

- **Experience Questions** – "what has your experience told you?"

- **Assumptions Questions** – "what assumptions are we making here?"

- **Beliefs Questions** – "what do we believe about the situation and how does that effect our decision?"

A major glitch we have in our thinking is related to our inability to make good decisions. We think we're rational, but guess what? Yes, you've got it - we're actually being emotional. Now, I'm all in favour of using your emotions to guide you, but let's remember, we do have a rather important cognitive function too – we have an all-important neocortex and we do need that bit too.

What is extraordinary is that we supress the emotions that will help us to function well, and pretend that we're being rational when we aren't! How on earth did we make it this far?

A good way to look at this has been demonstrated by Dan Gilbert[93] who reviews Bernoulli's Formula – a wonderfully

---

[93] Gilbert, D. (2007). *Stumbling on happiness*. London: Harper Perennial.

simple way of making the best decision every time! Yes, here is the answer – are you ready?

Assess the odds of gain x the value of gain

So for example, in a coin toss, if it comes up heads, you get £10. Should you pay £4 to play? Odds are 1/2 that the coin will come up heads, and the value of the gain is £10, so (1/2) x (£10) = £5. Since it would cost you £4, then it's worth it... Oh, if only it were that simple!

Unfortunately, we make two errors. We make errors in assessing the odds of making any gain, and we make mistakes in assessing the value of the gain. So basically, we're rubbish!

If you don't believe me think about it like this. What is more dangerous? A cycle down the road? A tornado? A terrorist attack? A ride on a rollercoaster? A swimming pool? Being asthmatic? Actually asthma and swimming pools and a cycle down the road are much more dangerous statistically than any of the others.

Odds of dying:

Bicycle accident: 1 in 4,147

Pedestrian accident: 1 in 623

Swimming pool accident: 1 in 1,073

Rollercoaster: 1 in 24,000,000

So we tend to greatly over-estimate the chances of us succeeding and under estimate the chances of things going wrong.

Then there is the second mistake – our errors in recognising value.

Dan Gilbert gives this great example – ask yourself this question and see if you have an inability to get real about value:

If you lost your ticket on the way to the movies, would you buy another ticket?

Many people would not because they have already spent the £10 on a ticket. To buy another ticket would mean that, in their minds, the ticket had cost £20. We compare what we are spending with the past and what we have already spent, rather than the value we will get from the experience.

But say you put twenty pounds in your wallet, and then went off to the cinema to buy your ticket to see a film. When you get to the cinema you find you've lost £10 on route. Now what would you do? Well you are likely to buy the ticket anyway – and be annoyed about losing £10 – but you'll probably still buy the ticket.

The thing is, in the second scenario it doesn't *feel* like you're spending £20 on a ticket. But in both cases the net result would be the same – but in one scenario you go and have some fun at the movies, and in the other you get all cross and go home and have a night in with the cat – and some bitter recriminations about how stupid you've been – am I getting somewhere close here?

Our first reaction to being asked what our experience has actually taught us is to think about what we have heard or seen in the press – but when we think about our actual experience the results can be very different. I may think that murder and mayhem are all around me from reviewing the media, but in my life I may not have actually had that much real exposure to this. There are people who do, of course, have a lot of experience of this kind of horror. We just have to appreciate that our actual experience is different from our imagined experience. And that our ability to measure the odds and the value of a gain are deeply flawed and may need serious unpicking.

Cognitive – Reframing the situation

Often the problems that cause psychological game playing that undermine your best efforts are due to low self-esteem, or lack of belief in oneself. By helping them to rethink, or reframe, the situation you can help the employee to look at it differently. Reframing simply means altering the context and challenging the perception by reviewing evidence and focusing upon reality, rather than their fantasy (of what other people might think, for example).

One great way to do that is to get into the metaposition[94]. In other words, helicopter above the situation and see it from afar. A simple way to do this is to imagine someone other than yourself, such as your friend Mathilda, in this situation, and ask yourself – what advice would I give to Mathilda right now? It is extraordinary how often the advice we'd give to our friend is the exact opposite of what we give to ourselves.

Other useful ways to reframe can be in fantasising about what other people may think – actually we do this *all the time* – only when we reframe we challenge the fantasies we usually run (you know this sort of thing "they'll hate me, think I'm rubbish, never speak to me again,") and instead try "well, they've probably got their own worries right now, they've probably done something like this themselves and know how embarrassing it is, perhaps they just want to be liked too" et cetera – you can come up with your own ones; and in working

---

[94] Rodenburg, P. (1992). The right to speak. New York: Routledge.

with others, you can help them to review things a little differently and challenge the current frame through which they may be viewing the world.

Worst Case Scenario

When you review and then accept the very worst case scenario – the worst thing that could possibly happen, it is a great way to relieve anxiety. I'm not saying that thinking the worst is a good idea all the time, but it helps get a sense of perspective, especially when your worst case is challenged and we ask ourselves – is this really likely?

Often, the first response I get to this question "what is the worst thing that could happen to you" is "I'll get fired!" But after no more than a second or two people then think about that response – now it's out there and verbalised – and will say, "Actually, I probably won't get fired". It's getting it out there, so it can be evaluated in the cold light of day that makes all the difference. We get anxieties about things that will probably never happen, and this creates untold difficulties for us, and for the people around us – as out emotions burst out in unpleasant ways – and this is where BLAME becomes a big factor.

Our limbic system finds blame a great reliever of stress and anxiety. The fact that it may destroy our relationships and undermine our integrity does not feature in its (not quite so) master plan![95]

Making the future happen

Once you have created a good grounding, by developing an emotional environment that supports commitment, by facilitating a sense of security and enabling honest self-expression, you need to look at what moves people from being transactionally engaged – the work is enjoyable – to being committed – they love the business.

This transformation happens when the employee buy into the values, goals and aspirations of the business, so the way in which you build the forward pathway for your team will dictate how committed they will eventually be.

Projective behaviours

As a leader you need to create an imagining of the future, by clearly conceiving this with the team and stating clearly what this vision will mean. This is all about how you talk about the

---

[95] Brown, B. (2008). *I thought it was just me (but it isn't)*. New York: Gotham Books.

future, and how you build this into every day communication and language.

As a team you should all be talking about what the future will look like, what you dream of and what you want to achieve – for the benefit of all.

Motive behaviours

Linked with projecting the team into the future is the vital component of the mission. It's important that this is done in terms of the benefits to the team, but also, even more importantly, in terms of the benefits to the world as a whole.

You need to project your team into the Brave New World, immerse them in it so that they can feel excited and motivated. They need to know their part in it, and how they benefit the team and the world as a whole.

The team need to understand their own drivers, and how they link to the organisation's mission, and that these two together must link to create a sense of "purpose". When your employees have a sense of purpose they will be well on the way to becoming emotionally committed.

Keeping on course – Orientation

Now you have created the forward pathway, you need to keep you team on board. And this means considering their individual needs. This is where you orientate your people. In other words, you align their mission and goals with that of the organisation.

This involves two behaviours: perspective and adaptive

Perspective

In order to orientate our teams to the organisation we need to consider how they perceive their world. When we understand the differences in the ways we perceive we can accommodate and facilitate their commitment.

The key areas that you need to consider are:

Time perspective

The way in which the team view their lives in terms of time – whether they be future, present or past focussed, will impact

*26 Watchdog
By Jazz*

upon how they relate to the organisation. Future focussed people will clearly find it easier to project forward in time, and enjoy working towards a goal, but you will need to adapt your approach to those who are more present or past orientated. You may need to help them to tap into their future focus, and enjoy doing so.[96]

There are six different time perspectives relating to the 3 aspects of time – past, present and future.

---

[96] Zimbardo, P and Boyd J (2010) *The Time Paradox: Using the New Psychology of Time to Your Advantage* Rider ISBN 1846041554

Time Perspective	Tell Tale Signs	How to appeal to them to learn and change
Future focused	Love plans and future paths	Easy to engage and sell future benefits
Future Transcendental	Present as spiritual	Appeal to spiritual values
Past positive	Likes the 'good old days'	Remind of how to bring back 'good old days', anchor good feelings
Past negative	Focus on past mistakes, poor decisions	Urge not to regret inaction, remind of times when no decision = regret for an individual
Present hedonistic	Enthusiastic, in the moment, not worried about tomorrow, talk about what they love to do	Personal benefit. Fun! Easy! Reduce workload so free for what you love
Present fatalistic	Find problems easily, but not solutions. Complain about lack of change, but 'nothing I can do'	Forget the new big thing, focus on preventing losing job. Caution! These people can exhaust you

27 Time Perspective, After Philip Zimbardo

Sensory perspectives

We all interpret the world through our senses, and we use language to relate this to each other. By listening and understanding the different senses that people relate to, as well as our own, we can communicate in a compelling way with them.[97] [98]

Beliefs

We all have beliefs about ourselves and the world. And among those there are frequently those beliefs that hold us back, or send us into psychological game playing. By challenging limiting beliefs we can help our team to unlock their full potentials and live their lives to the full.[99]

Adaptive - Keeping the dream alive

Finally, you need to create a challenge, without this you will not create the commitment you want from your team. Work should be challenging, it should stretch the skills, but not too

---

[97] Genie Laborde, Influencing with Integrity

[98] Grinder and Bandler on Neurolinguistic Programming

[99] Alok Jha, (2005) 'Where Belief is Born' *The Guardian*, 30 June [online] Available at: http://www.theguardian.com/science/2005/jun/30/psychology.neuroscience (accessed 2 September 2015)

much. It needs to remain within the ability – just pushing it a little.

In so doing the employee goes through a continual process of mastery.

During this they can achieve work flow, and this is an intense form of happiness. It is not like joyful happiness of going out with friends, or laughing at something funny. Instead it is the happiness of satisfaction, and it is a powerful force.

When you can create this, and ensure that your employees feel a sense of balance in their lives; that the challenges they face are not becoming stressful, but remain testing and encourage mastery, you will have happiness at work, a passionate and committed workforce... **and the ability to achieve your dreams.**

So to summarise, an A+B leader should analyse, model, create, orientate. And at the same time, being 'OK' about who we are, being mindful, and practising empathy are all vital pre-requisites of A+B Leadership

CHAPTER 8
The "magic formula" that makes people embrace organisational change

I'm always amazed at how infrequently those leading change in organizations consider the psychology behind it. Change is seen as hard work, we assume there will be resistance, and that the resistance is due to people being difficult, stuck in their ways and unable to see the benefits to the business as they are absorbed in their own self-interest.

Do you recognize those sentiments? Well, knock them on the head right now!

People are not resistant to change. They are resistant to anything that challenges their beliefs.

Psychologist Leon Festinger, as far back as 1957[100], explained his theory of cognitive dissonance. He noted that when people's beliefs are not consistent with their actions it creates severe mental disturbance. And as a result we have to do something; either alter our beliefs or alter our actions.

What I believe, what I value is out of kilter with the new reality I'm facing.

If you are asked to eat meat when you are a vegetarian, or to discipline a vulnerable person you would also have that same feeling. It's just wrong, wrong, wrong.

This is not awkwardness, belligerence or mean-spirited – it is a deep-seated psychological need that we all have to balance out the things that do not "add up" in our minds.

Our beliefs are fundamental to our sense of self. And when organizations appeal to what people believe in they tend to

---

[100] Leon Festinger, *A Theory of Cognitive Dissonance*, Stanford University, Stanford, Calif., 1957

have businesses that create strong engagement with their employees. For example, people who work for The Body Shop tend to share the beliefs of the Founder, Anita Roddick[101], at least certainly when she was at the helm. There are many examples of similar businesses – the employees believe what the business believes and so they are engaged. And interestingly, these organizations are often the most innovative!

Why is this? Why do some companies take their people along with them when they change?

Here is the magic bit:

Because when people believe in the purpose of the organization they won't just be happy to change – they will feel compelled to change because if they do not they will feel cognitive dissonance! Not changing causes them stress and is unsettling.

So, the first of my messages is that all organizations need to think about what they believe in – what their purpose is, how

---

[101] Roddick, A. (1991). *Body and soul.* New York: Crown.

they can communicate this and help people to understand and believe in it too.

And then, only then, begin to think about how to change – because, when your people believe what you believe THEY will be the ones driving change for YOU!

Cognitive Dissonance

If you understand cognitive dissonance then you will understand how to present and carry out change.

Many of my private clients come to see me because they have experienced such extreme cognitive dissonance that it has created a serious trauma for them. In some cases it can lead to Post Traumatic Stress Disorder (PTSD).

So what's going on?

Learning Curve

The process of learning creates discrete patterns of connections in our brains which result in specific behaviours. These are called schema. When we learn something new we go through a process of assimilation and accommodation – this means we assimilate new information into the schema (so we add something to it) and we alter the connections to adapt, so that we modify our responses and behaviour. This is normal and occurs all the time.[102][103]

The process of learning as an adult, however, is not quite as straight forward as all that, because it's not always easy to shift that schema once it has been set in place. And when we see something new that we want to do, it can look easy, but actually altering those neural pathways is something that only happens with **frequency, duration and intensity.** All three of which are **"behaviours".**

In other words, it's not just knowing, it's doing that helps to adapt a schema.

The usual pattern of learning follows a pathway that is commonly called a "learning curve. So called because it can

[102] Ginsberg and Opper, Piaget's Theory of Intellectual Development
[103] Psychology of Change 2003 MckInsey Emily Lawson and Colin Price

sometimes veer sharply upwards, making us feel as though we are climbing a steep incline.

There is another aspect to this process, and that is the emotional content. Learning is not a cognitive experience alone. It is also an emotional journey. The above diagram was provided to me by Lorraine (Rain) Hitchman of PSTA Ltd[104] and it provides a perfect analysis of the emotional as well as the cognitive journey we embark upon each time we learn something new.

Achieving acceptance is the goal, as at this point we are able to progress quickly into competence. Acceptance is an important and much under-appreciated emotion. Being able to accept reality, able to accept oneself and others as they are is a precursor to love – in fact when we combine acceptance and joy we create the alchemy that results in love.

A positive learning experience enables us to progress through denial, fear, anger and resistance, sometimes so quickly that we hardly notice them. But then we reach acceptance.

---

[104] Lorraine Hitchman http://psta.uk.com/

The "magic formula" that makes people embrace organisational change

The effects of cognitive dissonance[105] can be explained by imagining taking the same pathway to work every day. You walk along the same road, turn right at the same junction, scoot across the park and cross the usual main road at the traffic lights.

Now what if you took this route, as usual, one day and the office had gone; apparently disappeared into space.

You are told that it is now somewhere else, and you have to find it. It's so obvious! You should be able to see it from where you are standing. And yes, you can see it, but you cannot see a single path road or crossing that will take you there. Your mind starts turning in circles, how can you get to work? There is no pathway that you recognise. So you take a different route, and your heart is racing now because you are afraid you'll be late and you'll have to explain this. The more you try to find the right pathway the further away you seem to get, the building is right there, just behind another one, but whichever way you go you just can't reach it. The anxiety is

---

[105] Barker, Phil. "Cognitive Dissonance." *Beyond Intractability*. Eds. Guy Burgess and Heidi Burgess. Conflict Information Consortium, University of Colorado, Boulder. Posted: September 2003 <http://www.beyondintractability.org/essay/cognitive-dissonance>.

now rising in you. You either want to scream, or shout or cry. You want to go home and pretend the day never happened. Maybe you want to throw everything in the air. The person next to you is driving you mad. They are singing happily. Don't they know how annoying this is? Are they doing it on purpose?

Maybe, at this point you should just go home. But to be honest, you are so out in the middle of nowhere, even going home is difficult and stressful.

There is nothing for it, you have to ask for help.

You ask that annoying person who is singing. And guess what, they take your hand and there you are, back in the office – how did that happen? There was some kind of secret passage. Why did no one tell you?

The trouble is the next day, you know that there is a secret passage, but you just cannot find it.

And in a real situation you can even have a strange "out of body" experience where everyone appears weird, maybe like robots, or the world seems like something through the looking glass. This extreme reaction is called a "dissociative experience". You may have had something like this when you've been given terrible news. That feeling of disbelief that is so strong the whole world looks wrong.

Is this the best way to create change? We all know the answer to that is a resounding "no". And yet, we put people into experiences which are to a greater or lesser extent just like this.

The usual neural pathways suddenly don't work – like everything I ever believed, everything that I could rely upon has been pulled away like a rug from under your feet. Our brains are struggling to make new connections that create a sense of order. And without that sense of order we are less likely to have a nice wash of Serotonin over our troubled cortex. We are, instead, likely to have an intense wash of cortisol; a stress hormone.

This is my interpretation of what is going on in your brain when you suffer cognitive dissonance. And I appreciate this because I had a similar type of experience with my mild brain injury – essentially, I had a nasty concussion that went wrong – and rather than taking a couple of weeks to recover, I took 5 years.

The psychology that makes change work...

The term Viral Change is being used to describe the new change model many organisations are attempting to adopt.

For most people viral change is inspired by the way in which social groups have annexed the Internet. As usual these days, organisations are trying to follow the trends being set by "ordinary people" who just happen to know how to connect using technology. And as a result the idea of change in organisations has become associated with Social Media... that's a basic misnomer. I'm not saying that Social Media is not relevant or important, but I am saying it is only a tool – it does not create change that is viral in itself.

Change that is "viral" is the only real change – and when you look at the major changes that have happened in society – even before the days of the Internet – it is clear that creating a groundswell is what makes a difference. Business leaders have to change their thinking if they are to create change that makes a difference. Clearly, cognitive dissonance can either support or undermine change.

Here are three ways you can create viral change:

The "magic formula" that makes people embrace organisational change

1) Changing attitudes won't work. You have to change behaviours first and attitudes second. I know this sounds counter-intuitive, but it is proven in research.

We tend to think that if we alter attitudes then behaviour will follow, but actually you need to first set behavioural expectations, and as you do you reinforce the values that this behaviour supports.

For example, the concept of washing hands in hospitals has actually caused change by telling people to wash their hands and use alcohol rub. Now people will seek to do this...we changed our behaviour and now we've altered our attitude and so this now has become a proactive behaviour. If you want people to become proactive, then set the behavioural expectations and tell them why they are contributing to the values by doing this.

2) Don't use values to motivate people. Do you think that you are motivated by values? Well, we all do, but the research shows that, actually, we aren't!

The main motivator that causes real change is if we believe other people are doing the behaviour. Social norms are so powerful. And as a result we can, in error, encourage the very behaviours we don't want. For example, by telling people "65% of people have been too generous on their expenses – don't cheat the system" you are likely to create more fraudulent expenses claims simply because "everyone else is doing it"!

3) Make messages reinforce what you don't want. The power of negative consequences can't be underestimated. Research has shown that you need to spell out and make these "tangible". For example, only 20% of people weather stripped their houses until they realised that the size of all the small gaps in their windows were equal to a size of a basketball.

The idea that a hole that large was allowing the chill winds to blow through their houses altered this number to 60%. It's important to put a "negative" frame on it i.e. what you will lose, and this is more likely to change our behaviour.[106]

Awesome and Contemporary East Sussex County Council – Case Study

One of the best examples of Viral Change in action is at East Sussex County Council. Assistant Director Leatham Green has instigated a programme of change that answers the key elements of viral change:

---

[106] *TEDxCSU 2013 Expanding Your Perspectives: The Three Myths of Behavioural Change, Cross, J, (2013).* [TV programme] YouTube: TEDxCSU.

The "magic formula" that makes people embrace organisational change

1. Leadership listens rather than directs
2. Stories are created and re-told (also known as Tribal Story telling[107][108]
3. Behaviours are altered – altering behaviours
4. Values are reinforced
5. Change is initiated in small social groups and radiates out from these.
6. A loose tight fit (allowing autonomy)

I am delighted to have been involved in the Viral Change – Awesome programme with Leatham and ESCC and together we created the "A*+B*+C* = Awesome" This formula has been printed on coffee mugs that sit proudly upon the desks of those who have opted to be the champions of the new programme; Being Awesome and Contemporary. The people who wanted to be a part of driving this change in the organisation have become known as Awesomators.

---

[107] DePree, M (1995) *Leadership is an Art* Bantam Doubleday Dell Publishing Group; Reissue edition (1 Aug. 1990) ISBN 0440503248

[108] Peters, T. (2015). Strategy: the story is more powerful than the brand. [Blog] Tom Peters. Available at:
http://tompeters.com/blogs/toms_videos/docs/STRATEGY_Story_Is_More_Powerful.pdf
[Accessed 15 Sep. 2015].

A+B LEADER CASE STUDY
Leatham Green at East Sussex County Council

How do you make a County Council achieve high levels of employee emotional engagement? There is really only one good way – and that's through viral change. And what I mean by that is allowing the change to come up from the bottom – whilst being supported from the top. I use the words bottom and top tenuously.

I've seen Leatham busting some moves at an Awesome Employees conference as he reminds us of dancing man – the YouTube viral hit video where a single man dancing at a festival manages to create a massive dance party. The point being, if you stick to your guns eventually people will join and then follow.

Leatham's idea was this: that excellence will happen if you allow people to identify what is fabulous about the organisation, what fabulous behaviours we all want to see and then allow the people to drive more of this fabulousness. Starting off with a brainstorming session, where the employees coined the phrase "Awesome and Contemporary" to describe what they aspired to be at East Sussex County Council, the programme of Awesome continued largely driven for the people by the people.

Engagement initiatives galore is the outcome – cake baking competitions, post-it notes telling people "you're awesome", family picnics and a very different attitude towards leadership by the middle managers, who have learned the importance of "listening" as leaders; and of knowing oneself.

How did Leatham come to this approach? He certainly sees his childhood as relevant. Research has shown that early experiences in leadership have a pivotal effect on later leadership traits. For Leatham, his childhood experience of living in a working class mining family whilst coming to terms with his sexuality was important and character building.

Leatham manages to garner a great deal of loyal followership from his colleagues, and considering the degree to which he pushes the envelope of corporate culture, it is astounding that there is such as wave of excitement and commitment that attaches itself to his endeavours.

It is also very clear that Leatham is a great advocate for his team. He inspires people to find their confidence and challenges them to mastery. It is not uncommon to hear his colleagues saying things like "Leatham has told me I'd be able to do it, so I thought I'd see if I could do it". Praise and acknowledge washes around where Leatham treads.

Change is a courageous pathway for any employee, so to feel that one is actually driving it towards what one believes to be core to ones values is bound to success. Leatham has managed to create powerful emotional and cognitive changes in the behaviours and attitude of the employees at ESCC by engaging them in following him down the career path of fun and happiness.

Dr Herrero claims he invented Viral Change[109] and he has done some interesting work on this. At the time of writing this was not a registered trade mark, and in any event this expression is in popular usage. I think his work collects together work that has already been identified by Tom Peters.

And I like to remember that Affective and Brainy Leadership does not say "this is all mine, hands off" it says "look at what we could do together!"

---

[109] Leandroherrero.com, (2015). Leandro Herrero. [online] Available at: http://leandroherrero.com/ [Accessed 15 Sep. 2015].

PART 3
Neuroscience and the Emotional Revolution

*"Yesterday I was a dog. Today I'm a dog. Tomorrow I'll probably still be a dog. *sigh!* There's so little hope for advancement."*

Snoopy[110]

---

[110] Charles Schulz http://www.gocomics.com/peanuts/1958/02/15/

The "magic formula" that makes people embrace organisational change

CHAPTER 9
What is the emotional revolution?

The world has changed.

We know so much more about ourselves, about our genes, our brains and our behaviours. We understand intricate things about the way with live and work, what drives and motivates us and what happens when we perform at our absolute best. We understand much more about what makes us creative, what happens when we are being creative.

We are a long way from knowing everything. A very long way. However, what we have learnt over the past 100 years is immense.

And this is so exciting for us in the world of work, because suddenly our absolute happiness and wellbeing can be part of our working lives. We can be brilliant, achieve loads and be fully happy.

What's not to love about that?

There's just this small issue. It seems we still haven't grasped how. Even though the blueprint for this Utopian world is there before us, there is still a massive gap between what is known and what is done.

I still come across people who balk at the idea of emotions at work, as though we have some kind of choice about them. And of course, we don't. We should know by now that emotions are a natural and necessary survival mechanism, and that they are not actually optional.

Why a Revolution?

I've been trying to alter the way people work and live for the past 20 years; little, by little. And frankly, it's too late for this. The world is changing so quickly, technology is taking the front seat, and we are becoming more and more disconnected from each other in some ways, and more connected in others. But one thing that's for sure, we are still suffering for our emotions.

So let's start with a simple fact - 40% of all work sickness absence is caused by stress.[111]

I'm not going to beat around the bush here – if you are suffering from stress then you are suffering from a mental illness. Now don't throw your hands in the air in horror. You may be thinking, well I'm stressed but I'm not off sick. Yes, precisely. How many people working for you and with you are actually suffering from "stress"?

Mental illness, stress, feeling miserable about your job, feeling that work life balance is out of whack; all these things are related directly to our emotions.

29 Work/Life Badger
by Tate

It's no good trying to tweak the edges of leadership, we need a radical new approach. We need an emotions led approach. We need a revolution in thinking and acting. A revolution that does not break down the people or the organisation – it only breaks down the barriers to our human connection and connectedness; the barriers to engagement.

---

[111] HSE (2014) *Stress-related and Psychological Disorders in Great Britain 2014* [online] available at: http://www.hse.gov.uk/statistics/causdis/stress/stress.pdf (accessed on 2 September 2015)

Start the revolution

So if you want to be an A+B leader you need to become part of this revolution. Now they do say it takes a crank to start a revolution – and I'm certainly that crank! On the other hand I'm in good company, they called Einstein and Freud cranks too. They even called the lovely Anita Roddick of the Body Shop a crank when she started up her green (to hide the mould!) shop in Brighton.

Some people are quick to shout crank – they're just afraid of the change. But no one need fear a revolution whose aim is authenticity, freedom from concern and joyful work...but they will.

We need a revolution because people are still in fear about emotions; which is why there is so much work for counsellors and psychologists like me!

So become a crank yourself, yes be proud to be a crank, and starting cranking up A+B Leadership...now!!

What are the revolutionary changes that we need to see?

The most important thing for me is true representation. When 5% of the world is white, it seems odd that the majority of people in power appear to be...white. And male. Around half the world is female, so that is also a big problem. Democracy is not just about voting it's about representation. And representation is just not happening.

The economy that we are built upon is a result of the northern homo-sapiens need to plan ahead for the winter. The nearer we live to the equator the less we need worry about winter, as there is year round food.[112] When we drifted away from the birthplace of humankind, Ethiopia, we had to develop different survival strategies. This instinct to pile up resources for "another day" has led to colonisation, pillaging of resources, slavery, banks, savings accounts, and European Food Mountains and a few with massive wealth whilst many remained in serfdom. The drive for stockpiling pitched us man against man and woman against woman.

If we can't learn from this we're in big trouble. The need to make our winter stores bigger and bigger so much so that they may now hold billions for some and nothing but an empty larder for others is not just lacking in human compassion, it doesn't just fail us as a species, but it is likely to kill us off altogether, as we plunder the world, make our fellow creatures

---

[112] Zimbardo, P and Boyd J (2010) *The Time Paradox: Using the New Psychology of Time to Your Advantage* Rider ISBN 1846041554

extinct, destroy habitats and slowly make ourselves more robot than human.

Notions that differences between races give excuses for us to keep our powerful organisations and governments pale, male and stale doesn't wash for me. Just saying that employing a person of African heritage could be seen as tokenism undermines anyone who is not white. And the implication that "white is normal" and anything else is an "ethnic minority" may be true for the country but is patently not true for the world.

We are all black under the skin.[113]

Whether in regards to race or in regards to gender or sexuality I go by the saying of Sheelagh Whittaker[114], who claims that the notion that you will get the best person for the job if you don't have targets and quotas selection is just not true – people often get picked for reasons other than whether they are the best fit. Selection frequently will find an ok candidate or a

---

[113] The Seven Daughters of Eve: The Science That Reveals Our Genetic Ancestry Bryan Sykes 2001

[114] 'Why Sheelagh Whittaker has been 'a life-long supporter of quotas and targets' Written by Jacquie McNish; Produced by Claire Neary The Globe and Mail Published Thursday, Oct. 07, 2010 8:25PM EDT Last updated Tuesday, Jun. 05, 2012 1:30PM EDT The corporate director and former CEO explains why she's appalled that Canada has so few women in executive positions

compromise candidate or person already known, so this idea that it will find the best person for the job is in itself flawed. Whittaker says that people who don't do a good job should be kicked out, whether they are women or men and that until we have as many incompetent women as incompetent men on the boards of organisations we will never have true equality.

There is no notable difference between the brains of any humans. On average men have slightly bigger brains, but actually, this is very slight, and many women have bigger brains than many men. Otherwise there is nothing much a brain surgeon could tell about you – not your sex, your gender, your sexuality and not your race. So from a neuroscience perspective, knowing that the research says women are being seen as better leaders, and yet we are not promoting enough women to senior positions – i.e. women are not being adequately represented – suggests that we need to urgently act to remove the barriers that keep those who are pale, male and stale in senior and powerful positions where they determine the future of the world. And this is not a new idea, but it is long overdue.

In 1992 NASA administrator Daniel Goldin declared that the agency was too "pale, male and stale."[115]

Well, the genetic difference between humans and chimps is less than 1%[116], ONLY 10 times the variation among modern humans. So let's do the math, yes, the difference between one human being and another is.....0.1% [117]Now I know that sounds like a tiny amount of variation but I do think that, given the extreme example of the dear chimp, we need to realise that we really are all so wonderfully diverse, and while there is so much about us that is very similar, as I say, the difference between our brains cannot predict male or female, colour, ethnicity or sexual orientation, on the other hand we have so many differences in the way we are; differences that are genetic, environmental, behavioural and psychological not to mention biological.

Making sense of the Crazy World of Emotions

---

[115] Douglas, D. (2004). American Women and Flight since 1940. Lexington: The University Press of Kentucky.

[116] Wong, K. (2014). The 1 Percent Difference. Sci Am, 311(3), pp.100-100.

[117] Roger Highfield, S. (2002). *DNA survey finds all humans are 99.9pc the same*. [online] Telegraph.co.uk. Available at: http://www.telegraph.co.uk/news/worldnews/northamerica/usa/1416706/DNA-survey-finds-all-humans-are-99.9pc-the-same.html [Accessed 15 Sep. 2015].

Have you ever been confused by the way people react to each other - or to you? With the best will in the world, sometimes things just don't go as you would like, and your best efforts may not result in a happy, committed and effective team.

This event will give you some key strategies in discovering how to analyse the emotional environment and enable people to express themselves authentically and purposefully.

What are the key skills you need as a leader? And please before we go any further remember, that I am not only a psychologist, but also a biologist…..

To answer that question we have to start with the people you are leading… and the first and last message …

Everyone is different!!

The question is how different? And how does that matter? Although we share the same genes, so no excuses for stereotyping thank you very much – we have so many variations between one person and another, and so the answer is to treat each person as a unique individual – which, indeed, they are!

What is the key to being a great leader? It is the process of understanding ourselves so that we can understand others. With all this wonderful diversity comes the need for us as leaders to recognise that we are not leading "machine men with machine minds and machine hearts[118]" we are leading real unique, amazing and, somewhat awesome human beings. And every one of whom has something special to offer – if we have the patience and the dedication to discover what it is.

---

[118] Charlie Chaplin's speech in The Great Dictator. This is worth watching in its entirety Here's a small extract:" Soldiers! Don't give yourselves to brutes - men who despise you - enslave you - who regiment your lives - tell you what to do - what to think and what to feel! Who drill you - diet you - treat you like cattle, use you as cannon fodder. Don't give yourselves to these unnatural men - machine men with machine minds and machine hearts! You are not machines! You are not cattle! You are men! You have the love of humanity in your hearts! You don't hate! Only the unloved hate - the unloved and the unnatural! Soldiers! Don't fight for slavery! Fight for liberty!"

CHAPTER 10
Emotional Ecology of Work

How do we make an environment fit for so much diversity? Well actually, it's not as difficult as it sounds, and it's not as difficult as you'd imagine for different people to exist together - in harmony!

Think, if you will, of the thrush and the blackbird. They are both birds you would find in your garden they share a similar habitat. However, a Blackbird needs moss and twigs to create its nests, and the thrush needs stones and rocks to use as anvils to open snail shells. Both birds have different environmental needs, and yet both survive in the same habitat.

The important point here being that even though it's the same environment they notice different things in that environment.

This metaphor is related to the way in which we perceive the environment – what we see in it, what we tend to notice.

Coding the environment

Are you one of those people who can walk into a room and say "oh, what's going on here, hmm?" You know what I mean, the type of person who just notices things; the atmosphere if you will.

I'm not. Sadly, I don't really notice that kind of emotional nuance in the room, but I know many people who do. And just for clarity, just because I don't feel the emotions doesn't mean that I don't notice other things about the room. I can pick up on other aspects, such as the group energy, I'm just not so good with emotions. On the other hand I'm very good at picking up on anything positive in the room.

But what about these people who just "feel" when things are not right, or just "know" when a member of the team has some big news to tell, or can "sense" that a hurricane is coming. What about them?

30 Socially Aware Badger
by Tate

Well, to explain this, we need to consider the process we all go through of Coding the emotional environment or valence focus.

Valence is how attractive or repellent the emotion is. So people with a high valence tend to be very aware of emotions in their environment.

Research has shown that there is no construct in the brain for an emotion. Anger does not have a brain site, happiness does not reside in that bit of brain behind the eyes, and revulsion is not stored in a green receptacle waiting to be opened when required. No emotions are a response to a situation, and one thing that Lisa Barrett[119], eminent professor of psychology has determined, is that you cannot separate the situation from the emotional response. Her research has shown that everyone feels different emotions about different events, and to try to study emotions as though they exist in a vacuum is nonsense.

More fascinating stuff from Professor Lisa later.

The Big High

As a psychologist, and an occupational one, no less, I find myself talking about emotions with more frequency that I had

---

[119] Lisa Feldman Barrett - Valence is a basic building block of emotional life Journal of research in personality 40 (2006) 35-55

ever imagined. As my working life has progressed it's become increasingly obvious that emotions are such massive drivers for us all, that to ignore them is foolish at best.

When I first started out emotions were certainly a no go area. Now things are moving on, but people are in denial about feeling emotions. And we are still struggling to get people to realise that feeling emotions is normal and natural. Actually, they are healthy and productive.

And although the word emotion was rarely used in business in the 1980's we were allowed to feel all the high drive emotions – so it's no wonder that so many people ended up addicts. The natural dopamine highs were difficult to come down from – the drive was difficult to control. Once up we wanted to stay up – all night.

I spent a total of 3 months working in The City, and then reverted to working back in Sussex at my own (very energised) pace. That was not a life that suited me.

But that Big High was a massive driver, and we are still paying the price.

Workaholism is an addiction, and has the same effects. As leaders we must recognise the danger of allowing people to work at this addictive pitch, and ask ourselves what messages are we giving if people feel that they have to prove their worth by working over their hours.

If we maintain that only upbeat, energised emotions are acceptable then we create an impossible culture that will rely on unnatural means of perpetuating itself. And of course it is clearly not sustainable.

In order to enjoy the big highs we have to experience every other possible emotion too, as the "joy is not the same without the pain". If we are to prevent anxiety taking hold we need to enable the free flow of all emotions, even the ones we feel uncomfortable with.

When you are leading you need to be an emotional revolutionary – free the emotions, give them freedom of speech, allow them citizenship and see your community thrive and prosper in authenticity, better health and full emotional engagement.

How do we know what we are feeling?

The marvellous Paul Ekman has carried out some of the most fascinating research on emotions[120] and how we read them on each other's faces. In fact, he has coded every single muscle

---

[120] Ekman, P. (2004). *Emotions revealed.* London: Phoenix.

group utilised to make every emotional expression. This fabulous piece of work has given us the most amazing insights into our emotions and how we express them.

Dr Paul (as I like to call him – we're not really on first name terms, but I get the impression he's a "first name terms" kinda guy) – has been everywhere, including out into the tribes of Papua New Guinea, interviewing and finding out about facial expressions and emotions, and the thing we know as a result, is that facial expression and emotion are universal and innate. Wherever you go in the world people use the same muscles and curl their lips to make a smile when they are happy, knit their brows when they are sad and clench their jaws when they are angry – you understand this is really just a heads up – there is much more to it than that and his books are certainly worth reading.

Go to the emotional refractory and calm down!

Emotions spike quickly and go fairly quickly. I say that and I imagine many people will be thinking that actually, when they feel angry it seems to last rather a long time. Yes, that can be the case, but emotions actually do pipe down even when we are still piping up. And we all know that feeling.

Imagine that you have just had a row in the morning with your partner. You were angry because he or she failed to feed the cat. You get all heated and bite his or her head off, only to realise that actually, it was your turn. Now, even though you know that it wasn't his or her fault, and even though you know you have been an absolute nincompoop for raising your voice and wagging your finger, somehow you cannot find the humility to say "sorry". You tell yourself it's because; even if it was your turn to feed the cat he (or she) has been less than helpful "in general" and then you reel off in your mind the reasons why this head-biting-off behaviour that you have just exhibited was somehow ok...well maybe not really ok...but sort of understandable...under the circumstances...

What is going on? Why is it that you can't just say –"Oh Poo! I've messed up! Sorry, darling, what a silly sausage I really am!"

Why indeed? Well, Dr Paul[121] says this is due to what he calls our refractory period. That there is a period after we feel the spike from an emotion, when that spike is falling when, although we can cognitively know that the emotion was not warranted, we are not yet able to really feel that. During the

---

[121] Ekman, P. (2004). *Emotions revealed*. London: Phoenix.

refractory period our emotions are falling but they haven't completely left our system. The length of time it takes for us to get back to base is different for each of us. Some people have a long refractory period; others get over things pretty quickly.

A+B leadership Feel-Think-Act Tips

What is your own refractory period? Notice this in your team, and then remember to time your interventions at times when they are emotionally open – i.e. when it has run its course:

1. Leave them alone for a while

2. Ask: are you feeling ok to talk yet? Or would you like some more time to let your emotions settle?

3. Keep judgement out of it

4. Review what happened, including the refractory period. Ask them to consider how they could reduce the negative effect of this on the team

5. Take action to help support them in increasing their self-awareness (and reducing the effects of a long refractory period)

Moods are different from emotions. Moods can last for days and set a general tone, whilst emotions only last for short periods. Emotions change rapidly to deal with the changing environment and situation. The reason they can adapt rapidly is because they are a part of our survival mechanism.

What am I feeling? I don't know - you tell me!

Actually the heading is not that far from the truth.

Professor Lisa has studied emotions over many years and whilst it is clear that we can identify what emotion other people are experiencing from their faces we are not always quite as good at identifying our own feelings.

This is because we are programmed to recognise facial expressions. And because we have Mirror Neurons which have a very particular job to do. They are there to replicate the experience we see someone else having. This was discovered when a monkey in a lab was recorded experiencing the same neural activity on seeing a lab technician eat a banana as he would have if he had eaten the banana himself.

The Mirror Neuron's role is to enable empathy. So we actually have structures in the brain for this, yes! And these structures are more enabled when bathed in the hormone Oestrogen. Dr Helen Fisher has carried out some brilliant work on the four brain systems that we shall be talking about later, and she identified increased mirror neuron activity associated with oestrogen and oxytocin. Later I'll talk in more detail about these.

Why am I feeling like a jar of coffee?

What is this obsession I have with coffee? It seems to come into A+B leadership all over the place – and I don't even drink it myself! But the reason I mention it here is because of emotional granularity.

Emotional what? I hear you say – yes, that's right emotional granularity.

To be honest, I think that Emotional Granularity[122] is "the new black" and the phrase will soon be sweeping the nation, so remember that you heard it here first (if you did, of course) and also, let's be fair and remember that Prof. Lisa Barrett is the one to thank for this.

So what is it? Emotional granularity is the extent to which we categorize our emotions as discrete or broad global experience.

---

[122] Emotional Granularity – Lisa Barret https://en.wikipedia.org/wiki/Emotional_granularity

Some people are really good at describing their emotional experiences with different descriptive, they are able to give qualitative and quantitative analysis – such as "Well, I felt a little frustrated at first, but that seemed to merge into the anger and discomfort I felt, and then later I felt upset and sad." Other people are not so good at this.

For example, have you had a shared experience by which you were enthralled? Say you went to concert with a group of friends and it was a wonderful and mind blowing experience for you. Afterwards, when you were all talking about it you said how amazing it was, how uplifted you felt, and then how moving it all was, and the intensity of that moment when all the lights went down and... and... what did you think, you ask one of your friends and his answer is "it was alright!"

It was alright?! It was alright?! Just alright?!! Was he actually there? Is he actually alive and breathing? How could he only say "it was alright"?

Well, actually he could say that, and this is nothing to do with gender, that was just an example! We all have different levels of emotional granularity and our friend in this example is demonstrating this beautifully.

Some of us feel each of our emotions as though they are so many granules in a jar of coffee. Others of us have less discrete granules, we are more coffee beans, or maybe even like rocks or boulders. Some of us have an emotional experience that is lumped together, just like that jar of coffee that you left open (you know how it solidifies in air and you have to bash it with a tea spoon to break it back down to the granules again?)

No matter whether we feel lots of little different and discrete emotions or feel larger broader more global experiences of emotions there is a common factor for us all. We all see the environment as either:

- Positive or negative
- Helpful or harmful
- Threatening or rewarding

No matter what our granularity we are able to ascertain and agree what we believe is positive or negative.

And we are able to bunch certain emotions together as being broadly positive (happiness, acceptance, optimism) and we can bunch together broadly negative emotions (anger, sadness, guilt). We can all distinguish pleasant from unpleasant – but beyond that it's individual...

A+B LEADERSHIP FEEL-THINK-ACT TIPS

Notice levels of valence in your team. And what is their emotional valence? Knowing the valence helps you to plan the way you will lead and manage your team. Are they primarily self-aware or socially aware?

Find out by assessing:

How many words do they use to describe an emotional environment? Lots of descriptive and granularity may indicate high valence.

Do they differentiate between Arousal and Valence? If so may indicate a lower valence or higher Arousal Focus.

Read on for clues on how to deal with emotional differences

Diane Keaton or Woody Allen?

I'm showing my age here, but the film Annie Hall does provide a useful reference for the next little bit. So we all experience our emotions differently, but we can make some generalisations based on the way people score on Extraversion/Neuroticism.

In the simplest terms, Woody Allen's character in Annie Hall epitomises "neurotic" personality traits, whereas Diane Keaton (playing the title role) is a great example of "extravert".

Woody is anxious, fearful, moody, worry, envious, frustrated, jealous, and lonely. Whereas Diane (Annie) is an outgoing, socially confident person.

So are you more a Woody or closer to a Diane? And interestingly this will likely make a difference as to how you code the environment. We all have a different ability to code our environment, and this is called our valence. However, we don't just notice emotions in an environment, we may be very good at specifically noticing certain emotions.

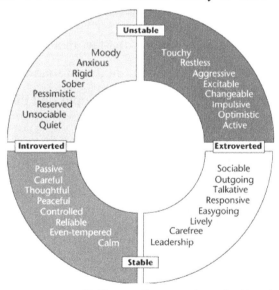

32 *Neurotic/Extravert chart after Eysenk*

Whether you notice positive or negative emotions will depend upon whether you have a high positive focus (in which case you will have a positive reaction to what is observed) or a high negative valence focus (in which case you will be good at noticing the threats more easily).

People who have high Extraversion scores on psychometric tests tend to have very strong positive reactions, so that they consistently report more joy, desire, excitement, and enthusiasm.

People with high Neuroticism scores tend to have very strong negative reactions—fear, anxiety, shame, guilt, disgust, sadness. And very often directed at themselves.

This does account for the fact that some people just take things harder – things are more infuriating, or scarier, or more anxiety-provoking. Other people find things funnier, more fun, and more interesting.

For example, the Extrovert laughs at hearing a woman talking loudly into her cell phone on the bus, while the Neurotic complains about it for days.

So we may find something intrinsically attractive (which is called a positive valence) or intrinsically aversive (negative valence) either have a positive valence focus or a negative valence focus. This could be an event or an object or situation.

Valence - How do we code and gauge the environment?

We have a standard set of values that say that sadness and guilt and anger are negative whereas, happiness and optimism and acceptance are positive.

We tend to have a bias towards threat – but this is not always true, and new research has shown that we have a tendency to experience emotions according to whether we have a positive or negative valence focus

I have a high positive valence – so I see all the good things, but I'm not immune to the threat... however, you can sometimes be immune to the positives.

A+B REFLECTION – FEEL-THINK-ACT

You are sitting in an environment now – an emotional environment – how are you coding this? What valence focus do you have – do you see positives, and help and reward, or do you see negatives, threats and harm?

This coding process is going on for us all the time, but social situations are the new ecology.

How do we identify our valence? People with a high valence tend to use lots of different words to describe their emotional experience, they may tell you that they can "pick up" on what's going on around them, and that they can feel the emotions in a room. People with a high valence are more likely to find an event highly significant and either highly pleasant or unpleasant, or highly positive or negative.

Noticing faces

People with High Valence Focus are more likely to detect tiny changes in faces before they become a fully formed emotion. This has been demonstrated in research, whereby people with high valence focus who were offered 100's of photographs of people's slowly changing facial expressions were able to determine earlier than those with low valence focus what the expression was going to turn into. These people are good at quickly coding the environment as either helpful and rewarding, or harmful and threatening. High valence people often feel sensitive to others.

Interestingly, if you present a high valence person with an emotional word, such as a negative word like "war" they are less likely to be influenced and less likely to identify another negative word.

On the other hand, low valence people are more likely to be influenced and find a word like "cancer". So it appears that the more you feel the emotional in the environment, the more able you are to identify it and the less likely you will be to be influenced by the positive or negative nature of random ideas.

On the other hand, high valence is also associated with self-esteem lability

Self Esteem Lability

The concept of self-esteem in organisations is played out as though we have a certain amount of it. Something like "Well Georgie is well endowed with Self Esteem, scoring about 85, whereas Ricky is around about 40. On the hand Pete is as low as 10".

The point I'm making is that we tend to see self-esteem as a constant. But this is not true for everyone. If you have a high valence focus you are likely to have something called "self-esteem lability", this means that your self-esteem can rapidly rise and fall.[123]

Why are some of your people so brilliant and yet have massive crises of confidence? Why do some people seem sensitive and need a lot of support and encouragement?

This may be a result of self-esteem lability.

A+B LEADERSHIP FEEL-THINK-ACT TIPS

Who are the people who have the greatest fluctuations in self-esteem? At times of low follower self-esteem:

Be ready to remind people of their past successes

Remind them that they sometimes feel like this, but that it soon goes, and that you always retain your confidence in them

Draw attention to their strengths, including the high valence, remind them that this feeling goes with these strengths and not to worry about it.

Get them to imagine a situation where they had previously demonstrated their past success in terms that will alight their memories – what was it that they can see, hear, feel and smell?

---

[123] Emotion. 2009 Jun; 9(3): 406–418. doi: 10.1037/a0015691 PMCID: PMC2949421 NIHMSID: NIHMS200475 Valence Focus and Self-Esteem Lability: Reacting to Hedonic Cues in the Social Environment Paula R. Pietromonaco and Lisa Feldman Barrett

Allow the memory to become alive for them so that it brings back memories of that emotional state.

Wait until they can really feel that and then get them to "anchor the state" by squeezing together their thumb and finger whilst they say out loud the positive feeling they are now experiencing.

Arousal Focus

Where valence refers to the pleasantness or hedonic value of an experience, arousal relates to the bodily activation that occurs. The more emotionally intense the experience the more relevant and impactful it is to us…but our experience of the intensity is likely to be different. Some of us are more likely to pick up messages that relate to our arousal focus. You know, I can't say this without someone in the audience sniggering, so go on, and get it out of your system!!

And yes, we may become aroused in all manner of ways. But when you are judging an environment emotional valence is only one measure you may use.

If you have a high Arousal Focus you will be aware of how you feel about something. The level of descriptive will depend on your level of granularity, but the actual degree to which you feel is related to the sense of activation.

What do you notice?

We know that both valence and arousal focus have an effect on the way we take in visual information and where we place our attention. Our eyes actually pick up on visual cues more quickly and readily when we have a level of arousal or valence focus – and if both occur concurrently we become very aware of our environment.

Remember that I talked about the environment and how we attend to things that matter to us. Well, you can see how our emotions can drive our interest in either positive or negative experiences.

How do Arousal Focus and Valence Focus differ?

First of all, if you are high on one you are probably low on the other. So if you are great at noticing the emotions around you in the room, you are probably less likely to notice the level of arousal in your own body.

Both arousal and valence relate to emotions. So we may talk about emotions, but are we talking about them from an arousal focus or a valence focus?

Valence focus is really all about reading the environment –
what is going on around you.

Arousal focus is noticing how activated your body is in the
situation – it's what is going on inside you.

Valence Focus is being socially aware

Arousal Focus is being self-aware.

A good way to think about the difference between the two is to
think about measuring anxiety and depression. Anxiety
suggests a high level of arousal – if you think about it the word
implies a lot going on in the mind and body, and heightened
state – this is Arousal.

On the other hand Depression suggest low levels of arousal; if
we imagine ourselves in a depressive mood we would
probably imagine flopping around or hiding under the duvet. It
tends to suggest slow action and thought, exhaustion and
inactivity.

People who have a high emotional valence focus are more
likely to rate these two the same – they are less likely to notice

a difference between feelings of depression and feelings of anxiety. The people are likely to say "I feel depressed and anxious" and it's suggested that this is because they do not recognise the arousal focus one would expect in a state of anxiety – it is all about the valence or emotions for them.

People with an equal Valence and Arousal focus are much more likely to notice the difference between these two and are more likely to say "I feel depressed but not anxious"

Cranking up the Emotional Revolution to 45rpm

How useful is this information to a leader? Well, I think very. All your followers will have some kind of propensity towards either valence or arousal focus, and if you understand this you can think about how to get the very best out of them all.

I remember the old days of record players and singles or "45's"! Yes, I'm really that old. Well these days 45 revolutions per minute relates, not to record players, but to leader behaviours.

In other words, we are looking to fill our minutes with revolutionary behaviour!

How do I start the Emotional Revolution?

In order to develop a committed and strong organisation and with responsible followers it is essential to lead by example – we learn from what is modelled to us, and the culture is created by what is modelled to us.

Whether we like it or not, or mean to or not, we will create emotional responses in others – so we need to ensure these are the right (A+B) ones.

As a psychologist I'm interested in what happens in our brains and bodies when we have emotions and how those emotions make us perform. I want to know which emotions make us perform at the highest level and what is going on in our brains when we are feeling and performing at our best. And do those two go together performance and emotions?

Well guess what – yes they do! Performance and emotions are linked. What we found is that only 25 percent of job successes are predicted by I.Q. 75 percent of job successes are predicted by your optimism levels, your social support and your ability to see stress as a challenge instead of as a threat.

Oh, do stop being so negative!

I bet you've heard someone say that before! And the whole positive revolution[124] is a great idea, but it has been poorly used. People saying be positive when things are awful are just not helpful, are they?

However, we also know that people who are happier and healthier tend to be more optimistic, and we are learn this ability to see the bright side.[125] This is a good thing as long as we realise that we need to be balanced. Being optimistic about everything is not so good, as we need to be a bit pessimistic when a risk is involved. Your threat response and your anxiety do have a purpose, just make sure you use them in moderation and at the right time.

The opposite of learned optimism is learned helplessness. This is where people tend to give up and believe nothing they can do will make any difference. This is just a schema or mental programme – you can change it. And when you do your experience of life (and work) is so much better. It is bordering on joyful! This doesn't do any justice to Martin Seligman's wonderful work, so I urge you to read his work on Learned Optimism and find out about his journey because he knows

---

[124] De Bono, E(1992) *The Positive Revolution* ASIN B00OX8IHPK

[125] Seligman, M (2006) *Learned Optimism: How to Change Your Mind and Your Life*, Vintage Books USA; Reprint edition (1 Jan. 2006) ISBN 1400078393

what he's talking about! And he is a lovely chap. Watch his lecture on TED talks too.[126]

Martin (Marty) Seligman is the founder of Positive Psychology a branch of psychology that looks at happiness, strength of character and optimism. I'm drawn to this as I'm not a clinical psychologist, so my work is not in healing ill people, I work with healthy people who want to be happier, more secure, stronger, empowered, adaptable and self-accepting. When people ask me "what do you do?" I say I help people to be happier in their lives and work – and that's how I see my job. It just so happens that happiness reaps rewards for the business as well as the individual. So what's not to love about that and about our dear Marty Seligman, huh?

The qualities of optimism and how it makes a difference to health and performance.

Mr Seligman came up with his theory of Learned Optimism backwards, as is often the case, from discovering Learned Helplessness. It appeared that when given negative stimulation animals and humans get to a point where they just give up – "it doesn't matter what I do, I'm always going to get this bad stuff

---

[126] Seligman, M. (2015). *The new era of positive psychology.* [online] Ted.com. Available at: http://www.ted.com/talks/martin_seligman_on_the_state_of_psychology?language=en [Accessed 15 Sep. 2015].

happening". But, the thing about this that got Martin thinking was this – why is it that no matter how much negative stimulation you give to some animals and some people they stay positive, they always expect things will get better – no matter how bad their experience is? You see, although most learned to be helpless, some never did. And this was the beginnings of positive psychology – the idea that some people are examples of excellence, and that we can model those, rather than focus on the majority or the average.

You can take Martin Seligman's Learned Optimism test yourself.[127]

Work done by others like Shawn Achor have proven that, yes, you can learn to be joyful and that this impacts positively on business performance. And the wonderful and entertaining Robert Holden (whose claims to fame are that 1. he opened the first ever NHS Happiness Clinic[128] – and to be honest we need them more today than ever, and 2. he proved you could learn to be happy in a TV programme where he took some volunteer

---

[127] Web.stanford.edu, (2015). *Learned Optimism Test*. [online] Available at: http://web.stanford.edu/class/msande271/onlinetools/LearnedOpt.html [Accessed 15 Sep. 2015].

[128] Holden, R. (2007). *Happiness now!*. Carlsbad, Calif.: Hay House, Inc.

miseries and helped them to turn their lives and emotions round[129]!)

We also know that happiness improves your health, and optimism improves your likelihood of avoiding a stress related death! If you think positively, and are emotionally engaged in your work you reduce your risk of death by 40%![130]

Later on I will look at the different ways your followers may present to you, and how you can deal with helplessness as well as other things; bear with.

---

[129] Robert Holden BBC QED The Happiness Project

[130] McGonigal, K. (n.d.). *The upside of stress.*

CHAPTER 11
Brilliant Brains

Now I can't threaten that I'm going to talk about neuroscience without mentioning that marvellous organ, the brain! I remember being asked once when I was only a child, what did I consider to be my best feature. My friends answered their noses or hair. I said "My brain"! And to this day I can't understand why anyone would answer anything else.

A quick tour of the brain

Now, as a biologist I could get very excited about the intricacies and details of the brain's structure and function, but what I really want to do is to provide something useful and easy to reference. So I'm keeping my scientific explanations as top level as possible (and I'll provide some meaty references for those of you who get excited as me about the science and those of you who are probably much brainer than me in understanding it all!)

New Brain - Old Brain

A quick look at the brain and you can see a mass of folds in the part we call the Neocortex. Neocortex means neo = new, and cortex = outer layer. This is the human bit of our brains – as some of the other structures (underneath this part) are older and even shared with other species like reptiles.

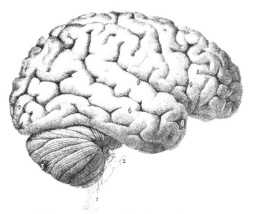

33 Outer surface of the human brain, Popular Science Monthly Volume 46, 1894-1895 (wiki commons, 2 September 2015)

This cortex is divided into two hemispheres – right and left – and at this point you probably expect me to say something about right brain and left brain thinking...sorry to disappoint you, there really is nothing much I'm going to say now however, the two hemispheres are related to different functions. I'm not going to talk about that stuff here. There's been plenty of others who have waxed lyrical about it, but it's not really helpful to us to explore any of this right now. You need both sides of your brain, and what makes you behave creatively or intelligently is related to the grey and the white matter. That's it from me on that today.

How we fill the Gap

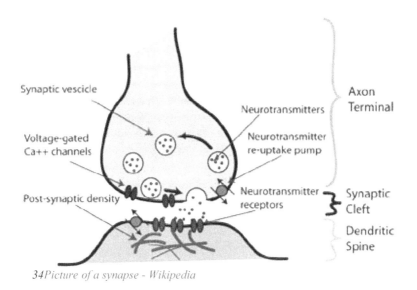

34Picture of a synapse - Wikipedia

The brain is made up of neurons and to understand how these work you need to see what they look like. A neuron has two jobs. To receive information and to pass on information. And the way it does that is through synapses. These are the gaps between one cell and another. The way a neuron "talks to" another neuron is by releasing a chemical. If there is enough of this chemical released it gets the other neuron all excited and it fires an electrical impulse off down its "axon". This is like a telephone wire (actually nothing like one but stick with the metaphor) and it can cover a long distance, taking information from one little group of neurons to another. This axon "telephone wire" is insulated – just like an electrical wire is insulated – to stop the electrical charge leaking out and to speed it's delivery to the end of the axon.

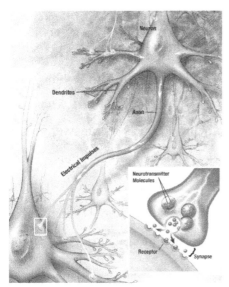

When it arrives it causes the discharge of chemicals. If you have a number of electrical impulses it will stimulate enough of the chemical to float across the gap (or synapse) between two neurons and if there is enough intensity of these chemicals it will cause the

35 Chemical Synapse schema. Source: By user:Looie496 created file, US National Institutes of Health, National Institute on Aging created original [Public domain], via Wikimedia Commons

receiving neuron to fire an impulse off.

Mopping up these neurotransmitters (or re-uptake) is as important as releasing them. It helps to ensure the correct balance in the brain.

The NTs can either be excitatory or inhibitory; some cause things to happen, and others slow things down.

There are two key Neurotransmitters and two key hormones that we will focus on are:

Dopamine: Drive and Pleasure or "The Reward Molecule" [131]

When you achieve something and you get that "yes!" - it's the Dopamine. This NT (neurotransmitter, to you) is responsible driving us towards goals, and so far it appears that dopamine transmission increases in every type of reward seeking behaviour, so setting and achieving goals is the answer – and so more of this at work please! The "achieving goals" is an important bit to remember. Goals that are too high or fraught with obstacles will increase stress. When the Dopamine is running round your brain you will feel more extroverted and a

---

[131] Bergland, C. (2012). *The Neurochemicals of Happiness.* [online] Psychology Today. Available at: https://www.psychologytoday.com/blog/the-athletes-way/201211/the-neurochemicals-happiness [Accessed 15 Sep. 2015].

bit of a go-getter. So it's useful when you want to make a presentation or be a party dude. You can get a quick fix by doing some high fives with yourself (yes, I know we're not all that kind of person) or standing in the bathroom doing the Fiero[132] pose. This is the pose you will see on my logo (for good reason).

There is no actual equivalent word in English for Fiero[133] but the closest you can get is a sense of extreme pride in yourself when you have just overcome an obstacle – not the negative connotation we can sometimes put on the word pride – this is all about feeling really good in yourself. What is fascinating is that we frequently raise our hands in that "Yes!" pose. This posture is innate – even congenitally blind athletes do this when they win. And it goes with a dopamine buzz.

SEROTONIN – relaxation and optimism or "The Confidence Molecule"

Serotonin tends to wash across our brain and is involved in many different roles. One key role may be in making us feel more grounded and confident. We know that there is a link

---

[132] Fiero – Isabella Poggi (see Paul Ekman: Emotions Revealed Published: 2003 ISBN: 9780753817650
[133] Body Language Success, (2010). *Body Language Success: Sincerity Secret # 20: Fiero Feels Good, Caroline Wozniacki & Our Mirror Neurons.* [online] Bodylanguagesuccess.com. Available at: http://www.bodylanguagesuccess.com/2010/10/fiero-feels-good-mirror-neurons.html [Accessed 15 Sep. 2015].

between higher levels of serotonin and feeling less sensitive towards rejection. This means you are more likely to do things that make you feel good about yourself, as you are less worried about what everyone else will think. This in turn helps you to feel worthy, and like you belong. I like to think of serotonin as the values NT. When you do things that line up with what matters to you, you will increase your serotonin levels, and when you achieve something that reinforces that sense of purpose and gives you meaning and accomplishment you will build up those serotonin levels.

As a family, we visit our local Retirement Home in order to sing to the residents. I grant you that this could be considered more of a punishment than a treat, but our dear friends at Marlowe House always give us a lovely reception. This little thing that takes such a little time gives some pleasure to the residents, and some pleasure to us too. Giving service has its own rewards, and one of those is the feeling we get from a wash of serotonin.

And the key Hormones are:

TESTOSTERONE – power without aggression

We so often think of testosterone as being the male hormone, but we all have it. And its role in your success as a leader is immense! Yes I mean it! We know just how much this matters from the work done by Amy Cuddy et al.[134]

What Amy's team discovered is that by standing in what they describe as a Power Pose for just 2 minutes increases your testosterone levels, and at the same time reduces your cortisol levels. What this means is it increases your powerfulness but reduces your stress and reactivity. Amy Cuddy likens this to a silverback gorilla, which has a similar hormonal make up – high testosterone and low cortisol. This is good for survival, as the alpha male gorilla needs to be powerful and in control, but being reactive would put those cute little baby gorillas at risk of being swiped into oblivion. On the other hand, the juvenile males tend to have high cortisol and that's why they are more edgy and could be more dangerous to Sir David Attenborough.[135]

Actually, this is very much the ideal state that we want as leaders, the silverback gorilla – calm but commanding, in control but family and team orientated; aware and present but not irritated and aggressive.

---

[134] Power Posing: Brief Nonverbal Displays Affect Neuroendocrine Levels and Risk Tolerance – Dana R Carney, Amy JC Cuddy and Andy J Yap 21st September 2010 APS

[135] *Life on Earth: life in the trees.* (2009). [video] BBC. David Attenborough in Gorilla Sequence – unmissable.

The study that Cuddy et al carried out is wonderful in its simplicity and clear outcomes. Getting your body language bigger and taking up more space is the answer. Get Power Posing now – adopt a Wonder woman style!

OXYTOCIN (and also oestrogen) – bonding and connection "The Bonding Molecule"

Oxytocin is a directly linked to human bonding and increasing trust and loyalty. We also know that oxytocin can help reduce the negative effects of stress.[136] You can give yourself a boost of oxytocin by having a hug, and it is often called the cuddle hormone.

*36Bearhug
by Jazz*

Face to face contact is the key here. When we look into the eyes of another person we get a rush of oxytocin, or even into the eyes of our dogs – which, by the way, also get a rush of the same[137]. Bless them! So you can have some nice snuggles with your four-legged friend knowing that they are benefiting just as much as you are.

---

[136] McGonigal, K. (n.d.). *The upside of stress.*

[137] UvnÃ¤s-Moberg, K., Handlin, L. and Petersson, M. (2015). Self-soothing behaviors with particular reference to oxytocin release induced by non-noxious sensory stimulation. *Frontiers in Psychology*, 5.

We also include estrogen here, and this is very relevant to the brain systems we are going to be discussing later – so pay attention, I may be asking questions. Estrogen is also linked with mirror neuron activity, so when we empathise with someone, it's because we can feel what they feel. Remember those little monkeys who could really imagine eating a banana? Well when you have high levels of estrogen and oxytocin you're mirror neurons are more likely to be working and you'll be really good at understanding how other people are feeling, and relating to them. Ahh, come on everyone, let's have a big old hug!

I was working with the wonderful trainers at Nottingham City Transport on their SuperDriver Course and we were looking at how to introduce the different hormones and their effects. So I went out on a limb and I showed them a picture of Boo and Sully from Monsters Inc. – Sully is holding Boo's hand and they are gazing lovingly into each other's eyes - and of course, they went "Ahh." When I put together the slide deck for the course they asked – "where's Boo and Sully?" because they wanted that adorable picture for their tough ol' bus drivers to "coo" at.

The thing is, they were right, because just seeing something cute like that, seeing two people (or in this case, two fictional characters), looking deeply into each other's eyes sets our own mirror neurons off and gives us a rush of oxytocin. Ahhhhh – indeed!"

Other Neurotransmitters that are interesting and relevant:

ENDOCANNABINOIDS: "The Bliss Molecule"

Probably responsible for runners high[138], these work like cannabis, so a healthy, and legal option for altering your mood state and achieving bliss is to go for a jolly good run.

ENDORPHIN: "The Pain-Killing Molecule"

The name Endorphin translates into "self-produced morphine." And actually look like opiates in chemical structure. They can be pain killers and are produced by the pituitary gland and the hypothalamus when you are doing a real work out. It is due to endorphins that you may "work through the pain" as it has that analgesic effect. Acupuncture appears to trigger endorphin production[139]

GABA: "The Anti-Anxiety Molecule"

---

[138] Raichlen, D., Foster, A., Gerdeman, G., Seillier, A. and Giuffrida, A. (2012). Wired to run: exercise-induced endocannabinoid signaling in humans and cursorial mammals with implications for the 'runner's high'. Journal of Experimental Biology, 215(8), pp.1331-1336.

[139] Wilkinson, J. and Faleiro, R. (2007). Acupuncture in pain management. *Continuing Education in Anaesthesia, Critical Care & Pain*, 7(4), pp.135-138.

GABA is an inhibitory molecule that slows down the firing of neurons and creates a sense of calmness. You can increase GABA naturally by practicing yoga,[140] meditation or mindfulness.

ADRENALINE OR EPINEPHRINE: "The Energy Molecule"

Here is the main guy for fight or flight. And when you get that rush it's exhilarating and creates a surge in energy. This is the result of the heart upping its rate, blood pressure changes so that you get the blood to the arms and legs for action, and away from the gut (and a feeling like you want to offload its contents – one way or the other!)

Adrenaline is really not one of the bad guys – but its friend cortisol, which stays around causing the long term effects of stress is the one to watch. Adrenalin can get you through that difficult meeting or make you a star of the stage.

Get your juices flowing – more about schemas

When a neuron squirts out some of its chemical juice it can create one of a number of responses in the adjacent neurons.

---

[140] Journal of Alternative and Complementary Medicine : study found 27% increase in GABA levels among yoga practitioners after a 60-minute yoga session when compared against participants who read a book for 60 minutes.

Neurons can be fast and excitatory – these are the most important and can travel right across your brain. Imagine a room full of chattering – that's your brain! But what are you going to listen to? Somehow you have to focus and this tends to be where a combination of different excitations creates an understanding of something. And this is where the elephant jokes come in too…so imagine your neurons pick up on something large, some others detect something grey, other neurons compute something wrinkly, and others note large ears and a trunk. From putting all this information into a schema you come up with "an elephant". By connecting other information around you, you can detect that the presence of giraffe and a savannah that this must be Africa and so it's an African Elephant. On the other hand, if it was *small*, grey with four legs and a trunk it could be a mouse going on holiday!

37 Mouse Going On Holiday by Jazz

My favourite elephant joke is appropriate here– why is an elephant large grey and wrinkled? Because if it was small round and white it would be an aspirin. Actually, yes, that's how our brain works, on collecting different bits of data and making sense of it according to a scheme it has learnt. It is the process of learning that links these different bits together and makes an understanding of it.

What is learning? Well we are not fully clear on what happens in the brain, but it appears that while we may make new neural connections, it is really the strength of the synaptic connections that develops in learning. I think of it like building A roads from country lanes. When the synapse has more weight it makes the computing easier and the thought processes find themselves running down these roadways easily. It's like they are easy to find, and you just roll down them like rolling downhill.

After my brain injury I had to re-learn some pretty basic stuff. I had to re-learn gestures, for example (weird, huh?) but I think the main learning I had to do was in how to focus my thinking rather than taking everything in all the time. This continual processing exhausted my brain and caused me to have massive time outs, such as having to lie down on the floor in Asda as my brain just said "that's enough! Close down!!"

I was told that this loss of my short term memory was as if the synapses had stretched and had to be reconnected. My experience of this was that I saw everything, and yet could not separate what I was seeing into distinct concepts. For example, in my hospital bed I could see out the window the exterior wall of the part of the hospital building in which I was, and a wall from a part of the building where it projected out, but in my mind these could not be distinguished from each other. I could not separate the wall near me to the wall across the way. I spent time, lying (in mild agony, mind you) looking at the two walls and willing myself to see them as separate from each other and not a merge of brickwork. Cognitively, I knew that they must not be connected, but my vision and my brain couldn't work this out. After some time, I was able to sometimes see that one wall was near, and the other wall was far and that there was a perspective difference.

Neurotransmitters can be fast and inhibitory, these ones makes sure not everything fires off or you can end up very unstable, they can work on a voting basis – whereby if most neurons are voting for "it's an elephant!", but two say, "hey, wait a minute, it's got four legs it could be a donkey" then the majority will overrule the minority (of fools!) and say, "ahh, shut up, it's a bloomin' elephant…obviously!" And thus is the role of the inhibitory neurotransmitter…gosh it's just like being back at school, isn't it?

Big dogs that want to eat you

There is another type of NT (that's neurotransmitter to you) -
the slow neuromodulators. These create a kind of "brain
mood". The excitatory neurons may shift you into action when
needed, but these are the ones that maintain a status quo – like
when you have your feet up drinking a cup of tea. If, however,
the postman arrives with a big parcel, you're out of your chair
and at the door in a moment – as a result of those excitatory
neurons kicking in.

Equally, or maybe, even more so, if you see a big dog running
towards you with the desire to eat you, the excitatory
transmitters will get all your flight and flight reactions going.

Now this brings me to a bit on stress.

To quote Jim Carrey[141] from his 2014 inauguration speech it is
important that you are able to distinguish the difference
between a dog that is going to eat you in your mind...and an
actual dog that is going to eat you!

Yes, this is an important distinction to make.

---

[141] Jim Carrey's Commencement Address at the 2014 Marharishi University of Management
Graduation (En, Fr, Es) https://youtu.be/V80-gPkpH6M

The fact is that whether you are imagining a dog or you actually have a dog in front of you the process in the brain will be the same. And the long term effects of your brain being wired up for stress are not at all healthy. More on that story later!

6 degrees of separation in your brain

If every one of our neurons was connected to every other neuron then we would need a brain the size of a football pitch[142].This may not be terribly convenient, and so for that reason the brain does not operate a "total connectivity" policy. Instead it works precisely like networking groups. For example, the social network site, Linked-In, famously operates on the basis of 6 degrees of separation, and even labels contacts according to how many degrees away from you they are (1st, 2nd 3rd degree etc.).

So what is this 6 degrees thing? You may know about the concept that every human being on the planet is separated from every other human by only 6 other people. In other words, I may know 100 people, and each of those 100 people would know another 100 people. If you follow the right connections you could connect with anyone on Earth. This is a

---

[142] Amthor, F. (2012). *Neuroscience for dummies*. Mississauga, Ont.: Wiley.

game we often play at home – we name someone famous and then see if we could find the right connections that would put us in touch with that person within six steps - yes, we should probably get out more, I agree!

In our brains we do not have total connectivity (everything connected to everything). Instead we have little local networks of neurons, and the occasional interloper that joins up with the other groups. Imagine a group of people at a networking club. You may know all thirty of the people in your group well, but you are also aware that Fred is a member of a different group, a club of plumbers and electricians. Fred could provide you with access to another thirty people if you needed a plumber.

Just in the same way as Six Degrees of Separation works for human connections, each neuron is separated from another by only six connections. And each little group of neurons has a neuron that reaches out to others. Like a little messenger. You know those people who always know what is going on in the other side of the building, because they happen to be best friends with the postman. Well, like that…sort of!

Hippocampus - The Seahorse for making memories

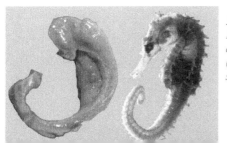

38 Hippocampus and Seahorse: By Professor Laszlo Seress (By email from the creator) [CC BY-SA 1.0 (http://creativecommons.org/licenses/by-sa/1.0)], via Wikimedia Commons

The part of the brain called the Hippocampus is important in creating memories.

The Hippocampus is so named because it looks like a seahorse – the Latin name for seahorse is, indeed Hippocampus: hippo pertains to horse and campus to "sea monster" – a slightly unfair label for such a sweet little creature). This little seahorse sits happily in your brain bringing together all sorts of different and disparate properties and turning them into memories.

The seahorse holds those distant memories of your past experiences so that you can use them productively in the future.

So this little seahorse is very important in learning. We need those memories to be fixed, and it is not co-incidence that the place in which this happens is right at the core of our emotional centre. I mean, if you think about it, the more emotionally intense a situation the better you remember it, right? Yes, so hold that thought…because memories, learning and creating plasticity in your brain are all going to come up as subjects and guess what underpins them all…yeah, you guessed it…emotions.

Our plastic brains

Yes, you can teach an old dog new tricks. Our brains are "plastic" in that they can change, and do change. Learning changes them. And you can alter patterns and habits if you apply yourself in the right way.

How do we know? Well this is a great bit of research[143].

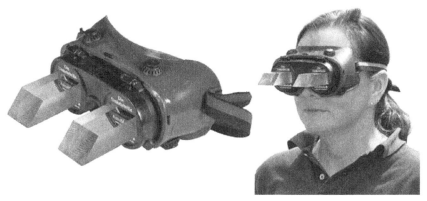

39 http://www.grand-illusions.com/acatalog/Reversing_Goggles.html

The glasses in the picture invert your vision so you see everything upside down - actually your eyes already see everything upside down it's your brain that makes it right way up. So some crazy experiments have shown that after about 15 days of continuous use of these glasses you begin to see the world the right way up – but if you remove the glasses and put them back on, you are right back to square one. But after 28

---

[143] *1890s George M. Stratton https://en.wikipedia.org/wiki/Perceptual_adaptation*

days you can take them off and replace them. And still be able to adapt.[144]

Can you read upside down? Try this as an experiment and see if you get better...

The thing is this:
The "cells that fire together, wire together."

Something similar happens in our brains when we learn anything new or practice continually. We create electrical and chemical pathways with our thoughts. As we think our way down these pathways we strengthen the brain connections. The more we travel these mental paths, the faster and easier these paths become, so that eventually our thoughts and resultant action feels automatic.

Harvard psychology professor and bestselling author, Shawn Achor, illustrates this:

---

144 Professor Theodor Erismann, *of the* University of Innsbruck *Experiments show we quickly adjust to seeing everything upside-down*
http://www.theguardian.com/education/2012/nov/12/improbable-research-seeing-upside-down

Just think of how you learned how to type at your computer. With practice it got easier as the pathways got more frequently used and the connections got stronger and faster. So much so that you can now type almost without thinking. Your thoughts and actions have re-shaped your brain roads. Through repetition, a good habit has become engrained and cemented in your brain structures and processes.

One of the most dramatic examples of this is a study of London cab drivers' brains that showed they "had significantly larger hippocampi, the brain structure devoted to spatial memory, than the average person's" [145]

A+B LEADERSHIP TIP

To make learning stick you need combine behavioural, psychological and emotional stimuli.

Behavioural – frequency, duration and effort

Psychological – values, goals

---

[145] Achor, S. (2011). *The happiness advantage*. London: Virgin.

Emotional – get the serotonin flowing for memory and learning[146]

So make sure there is:

- Repetition over a long period
- Keep the learner focussed on the value that the learning is giving them
- Provide clear goals for achievement
- Get some emotional intensity
- Include something physical like walking outdoors

Get the Creative Sunday Drive

Intelligence is related to the fast firing of the neurons in the grey matter. So what is this grey matter? Well it's the bit with all the cell bodies, the bit that picks up the neurotransmitters and responds.

On the other hand creativity happens in the white matter – or it appears in particular, in the cingulate gyrus.

We have 150km per person of connectors. These are like a whole set of roadways creating a neural network. Intelligence

---

[146] Kim Sung-il (2013) Neuroscientific model of motivational process. Front. Psychol. 4:98. doi: 10.3389/fpsyg.2013.00098. Received: 08 November 2012; Accepted: 11 February 2013; Published online: 04 March 2013.

requires us to have more networks, more connections. We need more biochemistry, more neurons firing their little hearts out, more brain tissue in which this can happen.

But what about in creativity?[147] Well here LESS is more. So the grey matter is full of networks, like a superhighway, you know, like L.A. or spaghetti junction. On the other hand the white matter is better for creativity. Certain areas of the brain are less packed and organised. And here the brain traffic slows down. It's like a stroll down a woodland lane. So you could say that there's more space for ideas to connect – and the process of creativity involves a kind of cognitive slow down.

So to take our analogy to the extreme: Intelligence is taking the shortest fastest route from A to B – in other words, taking the motorway. Whereas creativity is slow and meandering, a Sunday drive down the B roads and the country lanes of our white matter.

Doing things differently increases your creativity[148] as does telling your prefrontal cortex to shut up for a bit. Easier said

---

[147] Rex Jung - Creativity vs intelligence Jung, R. (2015). *Research*. [online] Rex Jung. Available at: http://www.rexjung.com/research/ [Accessed 15 Sep. 2015].

[148] Ritter, S., Damian, R., Simonton, D., van Baaren, R., Strick, M., Derks, J. and Dijksterhuis, A. (2012). Diversifying experiences enhance cognitive flexibility. *Journal of Experimental Social Psychology*, 48(4), pp.961-964.

than done – but his is a good reason for learning mindfulness.[149]

Why is it important to be creative? Well, creativity isn't just about painting splendid pictures –it's about being able to deal with difficulties and solve problems, it's about trying new ways and finding better ways. Being creative is a daily activity, and it's vital in this fast paced problem solving world of work that we now live in. We need tuned in and engaged people, and we need them to be active and brainy. Not anaesthetised by Ritalin and told to sit still and behave! The world is stimulating our children and young people and we need to respond, on the one hand by calming down a bit and taking our foot off the gas (you're going to give yourself a dizzy turn if you're not careful!) and by allowing their amazing brains to function the way they need to. [150]

---

[149] Wax, R. (n.d.). *Sane new world.*

[150] Robinson, Sir Ken, (2015). *TED TALKS | Sir Ken Robinson.* [online] Sirkenrobinson.com. Available at: http://sirkenrobinson.com/watch/ [Accessed 15 Sep. 2015].

Dept for Education and Employment, Dept for Culture, Media and Sport, (1999). *All our futures: creativity, culture and education.* National Advisory Committee on Creative and Cultural Education.

The emotional bits

So now I want to draw attention to those bits of the brain that are involved in emotions and emotional processing.

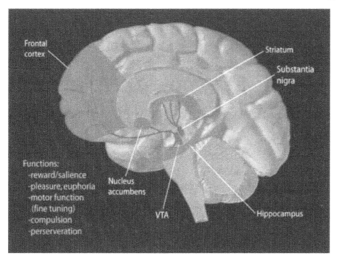

Figure 40Dopamine Pathways in the brain
https://en.wikipedia.org/wiki/Procedural_memory#/media/File:Dopamine_Pathway
s.png

The Amygdala Alarm System

So think of the amygdala as a little alarm bell – which can ring very loudly indeed. And the intensity of the situation can be measured in the loudness. Our amygdala is intensity sensitive and will stimulate feelings of fear or other negative feelings. However, this bit is not "valence sensitive" which means it doesn't detect positive or negative emotions it just detects intensity.[151] It's all about being r e a l intense.

The Pathway of Pleasure

The amygdala may receive a signal of emotional intensity, and this is conveyed to the VTA.

This bit of the brain, the VTA, responds to basic stuff like desire for food or...any other desires...but, the amazing thing is, it also responds to social things. It has the same intensity of response towards being given praise, or money or prizes or even to co-operation.

The VTA or Ventral Tegmental Area which communicates with the Nucleus Accumbens (often known as the pleasure centre). So if you are presented with something you enjoy such as a nice meal, or someone you have fallen in love with or even a jolly joke it will stimulate this area.[152] It's able to anticipate and gets the juices flowing in readiness! If you know what I mean...And so flows the Dopamine. Dopamine, the Neurotransmitter of pleasure and reward.

---

[151] Anderson, A. (2007). Feeling emotional: the amygdala links emotional perception and experience. *Social Cognitive and Affective Neuroscience*, 2(2), pp.71-72.

[152] Haber, S. and Knutson, B. (2009). The Reward Circuit: Linking Primate Anatomy and Human Imaging. *Neuropsychopharmacology*, 35(1), pp.4-26.

Dopamine works in two systems in the brain – the mesolimbic and the mesocortical. The mesolimbic works in the limbic part of the brain. This is the more animal bit of us – it's the raw emotions, and so this is where we feel the pleasure. The mesocortical pathway connects with the cortex – so it's a higher functioning pathway and is related to cognitive control, motivation, and emotional response. This pathway can code the relative value of the reward, and it can say to us "Oh go on, do it again!! That felt good!!" In this way we can develop perseverance for a task, we can keep on course with our goals.

The Prefrontal Cortex - The thinky bit

So we've talked about the emotional parts, but what about the cognitive thinking parts? The bit we're going to think about is the prefrontal cortex – this is the bit right behind your forehead – when your brain is aching from too mind thinking and you get a headache right over your eyes – yes it's that bit!

The prefrontal cortex does your conscious thinking, and it can only hold about 8 – 10 things at a time –if your brain is a computer then the prefrontal cortex if the microprocessor. This part of your brain uses masses of glucose – more than any other part of your brain. Whenever I send people off for lunch during one of my courses I always remark" go, feed your brains" I'm not kidding. You literally need to top up your glucose energy, so now, if you needed it, you have an excuse for saying I'm thinking so much I must have a piece of cake!

This part of your brain contains what I like to call the "control centre". Do you remember the Numbskulls?

Well I see brainy as the control centre – only please bear in mind that the brain diagram shown here is not actually accurate – as the control centre is in the front not at the back – and actually the eye department is at the back not at the front – but perhaps I'm expecting a bit much from a cartoon strip!

41 The Numskulls ® © DC Thomson & Co. Ltd. 2015

The Neuroscience of motivation[153]

Let's look at motivation from a slightly new perspective. When we think about what motivates us to action we may

[153] Kim Sung-il (2013) Neuroscientific model of motivational process. Front. Psychol. 4:98. doi: 10.3389/fpsyg.2013.00098. Received: 08 November 2012; Accepted: 11 February 2013; Published online: 04 March 2013.

consider that it's the drive towards pleasure. Or away from pain. Or we may think it's doing what we think is right. Or maybe goals are vital. Well actually it's all of them!

A number of things are going on in our brain – and this is the simple version of the story.

Dopamine in the limbic system is released when we receive a reward. This makes us feel good. This bit is also able to anticipate a reward – like when you see some mouth-watering meal or imagine the end of the day and having a nice cup of tea (ok so I have a very simple life, what of it?).

It also trips off dopamine in the cortical system stimulating the Dorsolateral Prefrontal Cortex (control centre) to want to repeat the pleasurable feeling. So this part of the brain drives us towards our goal – more nice feelings thank you very much. Also known as executive function cognitive control.[154]

There is another important bit and that's the Ventral Striatum, this is the bit that is involved in reinforcement.

Wrapped round the limbi system is the Anterior Cingulate Cortex (ACC) and it is here that we monitor our progress

---

[154]Kim Sung-il (2013) Neuroscientific model of motivational process. Front. Psychol. 4:98. doi: 10.3389/fpsyg.2013.00098. Received: 08 November 2012; Accepted: 11 February 2013; Published online: 04 March 2013.

towards a goal – this part keeps us moving towards that pleasure.

At the same time, the Orbitofrontal Cortex (OFC) is making value judgements about our actions. Now I see this as being determining whether the action will enable us to survive or not, in basic terms, but in a modern world our view of "survival" is slightly different from the ancient one. In ancient times we may have been thinking about avoiding that sabre toothed tiger – now it may be about avoiding getting the sack or annoying the in-laws. So this part is all about value and judgements and decision making. And it guides whether we take action, or not, and what kind or action we will choose. This part responds to "primary rewards" like food and sex (see there's a survival thing going on here). But it also responds to "secondary rewards" - and this is where it gets really interesting to us as leaders – money is one of these rewards, but more importantly, social rewards like praise and co-operation.[155] Lastly you will see my algorithm for giving praise – remember this bit of neuroscience – it will make it really clear why we should give praise, and how to do it so that it really works.

---

[155] Kim Sung-il Ibid.

In creating a dopamine environment which works for people we have to reduce threat and increase reward.

The wonderful Dr David Rock has done so much for neuroscience in business and he coined the term 'Neuroleadership' and is the Director of the NeuroLeadership Institute (I am not worthy!) He's also a nice looking dude – of course I'm not a Rock Groupie, what ARE you suggesting?!

Wrap up your leadership in a SCARF

Now if you haven't picked up a book by Dr David, then make sure you put his name at the top of your further reading list. And also make sure you fully study his wonderful work on reducing threat. Because he has made such a huge contribution to making neuroscience accessible and practice for leaders today. Dr David Rock points out that the negative effects of threat are undermining us at work, and that we need, as leaders to mitigate these if we want high levels of performance. And just to make that even easier, he has a mnemonic to help you: SCARF[156]

---

156 The SCARF model (Rock, 2008)

- Status is about relative importance to others.

- Certainty concerns being able to predict the future.

- Autonomy provides a sense of control over events.

- Relatedness is a sense of safety with others - of friend rather than foe.

- Fairness is a perception of fair exchanges between people

It's not difficult to see the common-sense of SCARF. If I treat everyone like they matter, keep them in the picture, give them some autonomy, keep the team happy and talking to each other and treat everyone fairly, and be seen to be fair, we have a recipe for an engaged team. Its neuroscience not rocket science.

The things we know about the brain that help us here are that the brain treats many social threats and rewards with the same intensity as physical threats and rewards[157] This means that the possibilities of being reprimanded, sent to Coventry, made to feel foolish are as powerful as if I said I was going to rap your knuckles with a ruler – and sadly I remember the days when knuckles were rapped and bottoms were spanked by head teachers with slippers, trainers and canes. And I'm not *that* old. And all the time, these abusive practices were no more

---

[157] (Lieberman, & Eisenberger, 2009) see Kim Sung-il Ibid.

effective than a decent reprimand. And a poor reprimand, can therefore be an abusive practice.

We also know that our capacity to make decisions, solve problems and collaborate with others is generally reduced by a threat response. But, if we are operating under a reward response our abilities are increased – we make better decisions, we get better at solving problems and we become the life and heart of the team.[158]

A major thing to remember here is that we tend to notice things that are threats more than things that will reward us. And that this threat awareness creates a more intense response and is also more common. We feel threat more intensely, we feel it more often. If we are going to make the best of work we need to minimise this in our business, working and social interactions with great care.[159]

Rock's SCARF model is made up of Status, Certainty, Autonomy, Relatedness and Fairness. These five domains have been shown in many studies to activate the same reward

---

[158] Elliot, A., Payen, V., Brisswalter, J., Cury, F. and Thayer, J. (2011). A subtle threat cue, heart rate variability, and cognitive performance. *Psychophysiology*, 48(10), pp.1340-1345. https://www.psych.rochester.edu/research/apav/publications/documents/ElliotEtAlPsychophysiology2011.pdf

[159] Tice, D., Bratslavsky, E. and Baumeister, R. (2001). Emotional distress regulation takes precedence over impulse control: If you feel bad, do it!. Journal of Personality and Social Psychology, 80(1), pp.53-67. http://204.14.132.173/pubs/journals/releases/psp80153.pdf

circuitry that physical rewards activate, like money, and the same threat circuitry that physical threats, like pain, activate [160]

So first of all we need to understand that these five SCARF domains are primary needs. In other words, we all need to feel a sense to know where we stand, to have some certainty about what is going to happen, feel an element of control in our lives and be among people who we feel we can relate to, maybe even like us a little bit, and of course, we need to feel that things are fair and just. If we can achieve this we can help individuals and leaders better navigate the social world in the workplace[161].

When you put together all that we know about motivation from a neuroscience perspective, this is what leaps out thanks to Professor Sung-il Kim[162] who is a Professor of Educational Psychology and the Director of Brain and Motivation Research Institute (bMRI) at Korea University. I love his work as it

---

[160] Rock, D. (2006). *Quiet leadership*. New York: Collins.

[161] Rock, 2009 Ibid.

[162] Kim Sung-il (2013) Neuroscientific model of motivational process. Front. Psychol. 4:98. doi: 10.3389/fpsyg.2013.00098. Received: 08 November 2012; Accepted: 11 February 2013; Published online: 04 March 2013.

makes such complex ideas so easy for us ordinary folk to understand and find useful.

Professor Kim has pulled together this model for understanding motivation at a brain level and has identified these three vital ingredients. Now listen up, this is very important for all you NeuroChemical Leaders™ out there. As always it is the magic three – and miraculously, it melds beautifully with everything you have ever learnt about psychology – only this time it is neuroscience. It is based on the idea of Generating, maintaining and regulating a motivation. For this you need:

Number 1 – You need a Reward driven – the approach

When we anticipate a reward and we start behaving in a way that we know will give us that reward our Ventral Striatum steps up and automatically starts making us feel good. We really don't need to think too much about this – the two things just happen – we anticipate and act towards the reward.

Number 2 – You must establish Values - the decisions methodology

This bit takes more attention. We have to evaluate the outcomes of our actions all the time – we constantly are seeing if we are predicting the outcome well or making nasty errors that will take us off course. Does this action meet with what I value? What will help me to "survive" in that broader sense? If we are going to continue and sustain our motivation then striatum is important, and also the orbitofrontal cortex (OFC) which is the bit that helps us to make decisions about value. So you could say the OFC is the values area of our brain.

Number 3 – You need to be Goal Directed – the control mechanism

Lastly, the goal-directed control is the process of regulating motivation through cognitive control to achieve goals. This consciously controlled motivation is associated with higher-level cognitive functions such as planning, retaining the goal, monitoring the performance, and regulating action. The ACC or anterior cingulate cortex (attention area) and the DLPFC dorsolateral prefrontal cortex (cognitive control area) are the main neural circuits related to regulation of motivation.

42 Kim Sung-il (2013) Neuroscientific model of motivational process. Front. Psychol. 4:98. doi: 10.3389/fpsyg.2013.00098. Received: 08 November 2012; Accepted: 11 February 2013; Published online: 04 March 2013.

A+B LEADERSHIP TIP

These two Dopamine pathways are vital to us as leaders, and it vital to creating a team of people who will go the extra mile, come what may, to achieve their goals.

PLEASURE - Nucleus Accumbens and Mesolimbic Dopamine Pathway – Praise, recognize, reward

GOAL - Mesocortical Dopamine Pathway – Goal directed and keeping on track with goals

Combine this with the Serotonin pathway which identifies the relative value of the activity "Will it get me what I want?" and you have a recipe for highly engaged and motivated people.

Dopamine Pathways   Serotonin Pathways

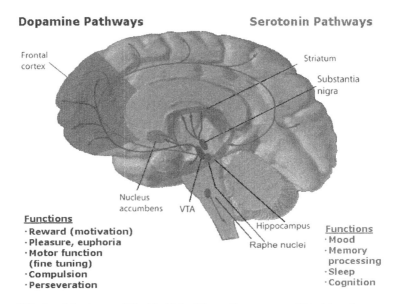

Frontal cortex

Striatum

Substantia nigra

Nucleus accumbens   VTA

Hippocampus

Raphe nuclei

Functions
- Reward (motivation)
- Pleasure, euphoria
- Motor function (fine tuning)
- Compulsion
- Perseveration

Functions
- Mood
- Memory processing
- Sleep
- Cognition

43National Institutes of Health, United States Department of Health and Human Services, or Wikipedia.org

PART 4
The Brain Systems of Leadership

"By the time I've grown up, we'll probably have a woman president. You know what that means, don't you?

It means I won't get to be the first one.

BOY, THAT MAKES ME MAD!!"

Lucy Van Pelt[163]

---

[163] Charles Schulz – Peanuts http://www.gocomics.com/peanuts/1984/03/29/

CHAPTER 12

Neurotransmitters and Hormones

The juices of emotion

Why do I say that our NTs are juices of emotion? Well because they may stimulate the parts of our brains that respond with emotion. We are going to focus on a few NTs and a few hormones in order to understand what is going on in our minds. And in order to discover how we can get the very best from ourselves and our teams.

We are going to discover how the brain system that we like to use the most can relate to the way in which we lead, and then discover how we can create the right brain structure for challenging situations.

There is some thinking that suggests that NTs were originally hormones that became specialised with our evolution. So there is certainly an element of similarity in the way that they act, although NTs work within the brain and neurons.

It's not brain surgery...or is it?

To be an A+B Leader you don't need to be a brain specialist! You don't need to understand the detailed workings of the brain. It helps a bit, but it's not necessary. After all, the best leaders in the world probably didn't understand neuroscience. What I love about neuroscience and all the wonderful new psychology is that it tells us a number of important things for us in helping us to become truly brilliant, and these are:

- The things we always knew must be right, can now be proved to be right
- The things we wanted to believe would be good are good
- The things that make us feel good, make us work better.
- We can change our lives by thinking a little bit differently

The things we always knew must be right, can now be proved to be right

We would love to think that being ethical, and treating people well and having good honest values would be a good thing. But do they really make us perform better at work? Are they not just a nice to have if you can afford it? Are they really a profit creating tactic?

Looking inside our brains we can say – yes they are important. If you want people to be motivated you have to tap into the serotonin system just as much as the Dopamine system. In other words, you need to drive people from what they see of value as well as pleasure.

The things we wanted to believe would be good are good

We all love the idea that being nice to each other makes a difference. We all want to receive a nice bit of praise. Well actually, it isn't just nice; it makes a difference to our performance and to our desire to repeat activities that result in us gaining praise. Praise is as strong as any other pleasure to our minds. Give us money, sure we'll love it, but that's because we want to survive and money buys us food, shelter, security and a lifestyle. We all need money, and we have to have enough of the stuff to make work worth living. Dan

Pink's Drive is so complete I hardly need to say much other than read it! [164]

The things that make us feel good, make us work better.

Now as much as I would love to prescribe a free massage for everyone, a holiday in sunny places and a gentle walk on the beach...this is probably not going to happen. But we know that these things make us better at concentrating. Yes, because we concentrate better when we have healthy levels of serotonin. Of course, we can find other ways to increase our serotonin levels, but we also need to remember that if we want our people to perform then what better than a little exercise, some time away from the computer, a bit of sunshine...and, oh what the heck, let's throw in a massage too!

We can change our lives by thinking a little bit differently

Oh yes we can. But it isn't as easy as that. We just need to use the right behavioural changes in the right way and the right time, and be prepared to persevere, and we'll get there. I do set out how you should set goals for your people to ensure that they reach them, how to train people so that they actually learn

---

[164] Pink, D (2011) *Drive: the surprising truth about what motivates us* Canongate Books; Main edition (13 Jan. 2011) ISBN 184767769X

and change their behaviours, and how to reduce stress and increase well-being at work.

What makes work worth living?

"Choose a job you love, and you will never have to work a day in your life." Confucius

Confucius said it all. If we want to make work worth living we have to feel the joy of it every day. This is where the psychology kicks in. We've looked at the brain, and we know how the brain responds (to a limited degree, I grant you) but we know enough for us to realise that:

- Our decisions and our values are related to our emotions
- Our emotions are a survival mechanism
- We are driven by pleasure, but that this can be as simple as the pleasure or being appreciated, of being accepted in our team, of being praised

Why have we built our working worlds on things that don't work?

Some of the things that don't support us are the very things we seem to have built our working worlds upon. I'll go further. It's not just that they don't work it's that they are positively undermining.

Ok, Tony Blackburn voice on now…

THE TOP TEN OF UNDERMINING LEADERSHIP PRACTICES…

At number 10 in the charts: training.

What am I saying? – I've made a good living from this! Yes, yes yes…but only when it is interactive, fun and engaging. Teaching didactically will undermine our creative self. Choose learning. And sponsorships and mentoring – these are great. And of course, training can be fabulous, but if it isn't making their eyes twinkle with delight then it has to go!

New in at number 9: meetings.

Endless, over long, talking about talking meetings. Meetings where people say things like "what's the heads up on that?" and "Moving forwards, what are our plans?" and anything else that you will see beautifully depicted in Twenty Twelve or W1A both painful situation comedies starring Hugh Bonneville. If you haven't seen them, then watch them with a notebook and make and note to self to ensure you NEVER utter one of those awful clichés! You know, I'm so exhausted just thinking about this, I don't think I'll say anything more.

Number 8: Scripts.

"Good morning and how are you today?" Or maybe "Have a nice day" if we hark back to the 1980's. You may think that by being prescriptive about the way your people act it will improve service and make your business loads more money – err, wrong! The more you constrain people with tight scripts and no room for self-expression the more you suppress their emotional selves. That's a good thing, yeah? No, no no, of course not – haven't you been paying attention? Their emotions are their barometers – not only of their own feelings and emotional state, but also of the environment and the people with whom they are communicating. When your people are free to communicate from the heart THEN you will see real engagement with customers and colleagues. [165]

A surprise entry at number 7: Disciplinary meetings.

How can we possibly go on without disciplinaries? In my view the actual number of times you really need to move someone

---

[165] MacLeod and Clarke (2011) *Engaging for Success* [online] Available at http://www.engageforsuccess.org/wp-content/uploads/2012/09/file52215.pdf

into the disciplinary process is very rare. And yes, you need these procedures by law, but my experience is that they are used as management methods, ways of keeping people "behaving". If people are not behaving in a reasonable manner then maybe there is a tiny little engagement issue here. The more we tighten our grip the more we lose control. I want a world of work where empowered people are able to perform – are allowed to perform to their best. Show me an employee who comes to work thinking "I think I'll have a really bad day to day, that'll teach them" and I'll show you some poor leadership. Yes really. Followers will follow leaders – you shouldn't need to beat them into line. That is not, by definition, a follower. That's a minion.

Straight in at number 6: "Be strong".

Yes that old message that we were given by our parents that we feel some kind of misguided duty to pass on to the rest of the world. Buck up, wipe your tears, and don't show any emotion. When I was a Practice Manager I used to instruct my staff that when they felt a little twinge, perhaps in their stomachs or wherever else they recognised that feeling of discomfort they should come to get me, take a time out and I would deal with the patient concerned. It was so difficult to actually get people to feel that it was alright to trust that feeling alone. I knew that if they didn't they would eventually explode one way or another. No, no, no to suppressing how we feel.

Hot on the heels of "Be Strong" a new entry at number 5 by "Explain how you feel"

So it's not enough that we have an emotion that exists in the part of our brain that has no capacity for language, oh no. we are expected to put that feeling into rational and meaningful words. Impossible. But we still expect people to do it – and stay engaged and healthy. Derr…

At number 4 a re-entry, reclimbing the charts, that old chestnut: Bonuses

If you think that bonuses work then think on. Yes, small bonuses can be motivational, but the bigger the bonus the less it improves performance. So thinking that a bonus will buy you high levels of engagement – forget it. Pay properly, and acknowledge people. A simple and winning formula.[166]

At Number 3: Appraisal Systems.

---

[166] I refer you back to Dan Pink – he should be doing good business from this!

Yes I'm going out on a limb on this one. I've been a slave to the appraisal just like everyone else, but I've now decided that at my company they are no more! Can you imagine how disappointed the people at MPC were when they heard this? Yeah, not actually disappointed at all. Instead we have regular meetings which we record fairly informally, and anyone is entitled to a meeting whenever they like in order to **give feedback** to us as a business. And we promise to listen, and act as best we can. Now doesn't that feel better?

Bang in at number 2 – Micromanagement.

Anything that implies some kind of micromanagement – this creates a threat response and therefore reduces our ability to learn, to be creative and to co-operate! This includes in your face management, checking, monitoring and overly tight procedures.[167]

And here, at the top spot, a slow climber... number 1 is: Blame

---

[167] Lob-ban et al. (1998) found that supervisory styles (in terms of providing direction and communicating with employees) may play a more dominant role in the stress process and suggest that supervisory relationships, have significant additional influence on occupational stress that cannot be explained by the role or demand other models.

Top of the pops in my chart of undermining people is using blame as an excuse for accountability. No they are not the same thing! Blame is, according to Brene Brown[168], simply a discharge of discomfort and pain. We see the situation, it makes us uncomfortable, maybe angry, upset, scared. So we launch into whose fault is this? I might add that Brene says that people who blame are inversely correlated with an inability to have the grit and determination to hold people to account. So blame is not good for leadership, it won't help you to achieve – and so it's about time you stopped doing it. Yes, you! I always knew you were the problem...oops, sorry, unfettered blaming burst forth. Is there room for me in your group, Brene? My name is Maria Paviour and I can also be a Blamer...[169]

---

[168] Brown, B. *The Gifts Of Imperfection.* Center City, Minn.: Hazelden, 2010. Print.

[169] RSA Short Brown, B – Blame www.youtube.com/watch?v=RZWf2_2L2v8

CHAPTER 13
The Vital Role of Feedback

W e all know that we sometimes have to deliver bad news as a leader. Sometimes we have to broach those difficult conversations around performance or attitude. Ugh, it's the worst bit of leadership, right? Who would want to burst somebody's bubble?

We all crave acceptance – remember David Rock's SCARF model and the importance of Relatedness? And this resonates with Bill Reddin's model of leadership which calls for, none other than "relatedness" (anyone would think these guys had been talking!)

Now if you think back to the Emotion Wheel you may also remember that acceptance is a positive emotion, and feeling accepted for who we are is the best feeling. In fact, remembering back, acceptance and joy is...love. So the whole idea that we need to be unconditional in our acceptance of people is absolutely vital. This is a psychological structure and premise, but it works with the neuroscience too.

So somehow you need to be able to give feedback when things are good, and when they're bad. And there is a neuro-chemical way of doing so: Hurrah! Ok maybe hurrah is going a bit far, but actually, the great thing about this is that rather than being the bad guy you end up being the good guy whether you are delivering praise or reprimand.

How so? I hear you ask. Well, like this: the structure shown in the algorithm here shows you how. It's been developed from Transactional Analysis models, Blanchard's one minute approach and I've added some neuroscience. In this way you get the response you want, which is more of the good stuff and less of the not so good stuff (or even bad stuff).

So, whether you are going to praise or reprimand the process is very similar.

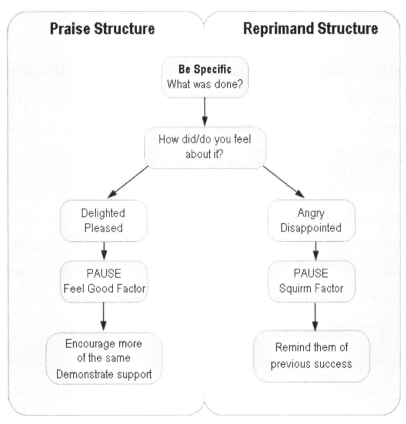

44Praise Reprimand Process, © Maria Paviour 2015

Here is an example of Praise:

1. Be Specific in your praise – tell the person what they have done such as "you wrote a letter to King Paul about the new carpets, and it was absolutely brilliant in describing

them in lucid detail, so much so I could feel them under my feet! Fantastic!"

2. Tell them how you feel about it – use emotional words (you need to develop your emotional vocabulary for this) I felt really pleased (hmm, its ok but a bit unimaginative) I felt thrilled, delighted, over the moon, chuffed to bits, excited, fabulous, relaxed, satisfied, super-happy…etc.

3. What happens next is key. You wait. Yes you just wait until they respond non-verbally – it will happen, believe me, usually a nod of the head as it sinks in, and a smile. We call this the feel good factor. Wait for it, because this is where the dopamine is washing through the brain. Don't miss this bit out – or your praise will not mean very much – wait for this bit and they will adore you forever (no promises).

4. Now, this is your chance to reinforce this behaviour. This will ensure you get the good stuff happening all the time. Just something like "Keep up the good work" will do – you decide.

5. I like a physical demonstration where possible, like a handshake, fist bump or whatever, I'm not a high five kind of gal, and I'm only just getting into the fist bumping thing, but you can use something that works for you and

the person concerned. If you're huggy and they are too, then hug, why not?

And here is the Reprimand:

1. Be Specific in your reprimand or corrective feedback – tell the person what it is they've done such as "you wrote a letter to King Paul about the new carpets, and it had twenty three different typographical errors"

2. Tell them how you feel about it – use emotional words (you need to develop your emotional vocabulary for this) I felt unhappy (hmm, its ok but also a bit unimaginative) I felt fed up, annoyed, perplexed, confused, stressed, disorientated, nervous, saddened or the most powerful of all …disappointed.

3. This time, the key moment is the squirm factor. You will know when the message has hit home as they will shift position. This means you've piqued their values in their brains. This will tell them this is not good for getting what you want.

4. So finish with reminding them of their previous successes "the last letter to King Paul was brilliant" use a previous praise for this and then finish with "let's have more of that good stuff".

5. And a physical demonstration? Well you see what you think would be right at the time. It's about what feels comfortable for you both, but I do like a pat on the shoulder or something that says that we still hold them in high esteem, even if they can't spell for toffee (that's what spellcheck is for).

Given the process I've just described it's important to note that you cannot give a reprimand before you have given a praise (or the structure thing won't work). This is good discipline for a leader – it means that until you've been able to see and prove that they are able to do the job they can't be reprimanded for it. No, they need training and support, mentoring and encouragement. You cannot reprimand if they are still learning. That would be detrimental on many levels. Not least of which messing up the dopamine process. We will prevent them anticipating a reward for good behaviour if they don't know what good behaviour is.

This also takes us to the problem of threat.

Working environments can so often be awash with threat, causing cortisol levels to run riot. We cannot make good decisions when we have high cortisol levels. We can't solve problems well. We can't even work well in a team.

So if we persist in creating a threat through our management and leadership techniques we have nobody to blame but ourselves when people don't perform.

The worst thing you can say to an engaged employee

I don't think that I've ever said "I felt cross" when delivering a "reprimand". I think the worst I've ever said is "I was disappointed" – and there are reasons for this.

Firstly, I have hardly ever delivered a reprimand – yes once or twice, but very infrequently indeed. This is because mistakes are part of learning, and I take that view when things go wrong. Sometimes, people forget things or do things they shouldn't have, but I find that when you have an essentially well engaged team you don't need to say a thing – you just need to say "what happened about…" And they already have given themselves a hard time about it. I often find it's my job to make them remember that they are valued and that this all part of our learning as a team.

So when I come to be "disappointed" it's usually a biggy.

Secondly, the important thing about allowing mistakes and not getting on people's case about their human errors is the overall emotional environment that this fosters. When people know you, as a leader, tolerate their errors, they feel more comfortable about 'fessing up to them. This facilitates honesty at work.

And thirdly, when there is an atmosphere of honesty and tolerance something amazing happens – people no longer feel that pervasive sense of threat, and start communicating freely. The best thing about this is that your team begin to give you feedback about your leadership. Yes, you heard me right, the BEST thing. When we can get our ego out of the way for a moment or two!

Watch out for the Ego

I love to get feedback from my team, and it is a real privilege when they do. I see this as me being successful – if my team can be honest, and think of the good of the team and business over their hierarchical position to me, then I must be getting something right somewhere along the line (even if they're about to tell me I'm getting it wrong!)

It's easy to slip into ego, and when offered a suggestion fall into the "yes but," game – yes I do find myself doing this sometimes – rather than allowing oneself to be open minded.

When I was working as Business Manager of a medical centre I did have to occasionally deal with issues of attitude – rather than learning. On one occasion it was a matter of a breach of confidentiality of medical information. The expectation was that I would give a reprimand, but actually, I only needed to say what had happened – my team member then did the rest of the work for herself. My job was to encourage her to be kind to herself, accept that it was a terrible error, and work at fixing the issue and preventing a repeat.

Another time I was all set ready to give some very stern feedback to an administrator called Jacky. I spoke to one of my managers, Bella, and told her that I was going to effectively read Jacky the riot act, she had failed to work with her manager and was irritated and vocal with the rest of the team about how things were not working. Bella was a very forthright person, but also quite timid. She listened. And then she suggested that I may want to consider Jacky's personal circumstances before I gave her this feedback.

I was determined that I was right. Oh dear, ego at work.

However, I did think about Bella's suggestion, and I wondered what exactly I was going to gain by criticising Jacky. Would it achieve what I wanted? And of course, the answer was "no". I was rationalising my desire to blame Jacky. And then I considered what would happen if I cooled off from being personally affronted by her criticisms and just dealt with what would make everything work better. Ah yes, the obvious answer – but difficult when we are caught up in our own emotions.

So, I completely rethought my approach. Instead of being critical, I looked at how we could deal with some of the problems we had, what support Jacky needed, and how we could build better relationships with other team members for this purpose.

What a surprise! We had a very constructive and pleasant meeting. We dealt with the real issues and we both felt good about it. We agreed to involve her manager and brainstorm some solutions. Jacky left the meeting looking better than she had for some time – I think the threat response that was driving her behaviour was taking a time out.

Later, I spoke to Bella and I told her that I had taken her sage advice, and rethought my approach. I explained what I had done and how it had gone. I also made sure I thanked her for giving me such invaluable feedback. Bella immediately responded by saying she hadn't intended to advise me. Of course I realised that Bella would not have considered it was her place to tell me what to do – but you know, actually it is her place. It's the place of every member of our team to tell us what we should do. And it's our place to decide.

The Magic bit of taking one for the team.

Being a leader means making the ultimate decisions and dealing with the consequences – good and bad. It means taking it on the chin when things don't work, and giving credit to the team when it does.

It's simple – but we can find ourselves emotionally struggling against this. Why, oh, why should I always have to be the one who is accountable, and why can't I get the glory? You may be saying (secretly to yourself). Here is the magic bit:

Glory is over-rated. Ok that's not the magic bit so please keep reading and don't throw the book into the corner right now.

What I mean is this – when we help someone, when we see them get what they want, well, it gives us such a wonderful feel-good moment. Think about buying gifts for people – at their birthday or at the festival of your preference. Don't you just get that warm fuzzy feeling?

Feeling warm and fuzzy

I love that scene in "About a Boy" by Nick Hornby[170] which was made into a wonderful film in 2002 starring Hugh Grant, Nicholas Hoult and Rachel Weisz. I'm going to go out on a limb here and say, to me this is an example of a perfect film! It works the movie magic for me. Anyhow, the point being that our hero, Will, tries to live an unemotionally engaged life, but when he is among a (albeit odd) family he begins to defrost and finds real joy in the simple acts of sharing. Ahhh!

Yes, and…there is a serious point here. We know that we can get really strong dopamine fixes from this kind of thing. Social contact gives us a reward hit, as does gratitude and giving. Remember, service is the most enduring form of happiness.[171]

So for me it's a no brainer to take full responsibility for the bad things and give full credit for the good things.

---

[170] Hornby, N. (2002). *About a boy.* London: Penguin.

[171] Martin Seligman Ibid.

And the warm fuzzy feeling you will get from your team's happiness, from them feeling loved and protected by you, will be as good as watching "About a Boy".

And the rewards go further, because a team that feels secure and engaged will be a top performer.

Yes, you'll get reward in the end, my child.

How we can get it so very wrong

Let's go a bit further and look at how we can get things really wrong, when we think we are getting the right. Ever been in that position? Or is it just me?

This is the OK Corral[172]and it relates to how we feel about ourselves and others. This is the model of self-acceptance – when we accept ourselves and others we are in the green healthy box – Yay! But we can slip into the other positions. We can become hopeless, helpless or defensive. When we are in the top right box we are "can do" and feel empowered!

	You're Ok with me	
I'm OK with me	I'm NOT OK You're OK *One-down position* Attitude: Get away from State: Helpless	**I'm OK** **You're OK** *Healthy position* Attituide:Get on with State: Happy
I'm not OK with me	I'm NOT Ok You're NOT OK *Hopeless position* Attitude: Get nowhere with State: Hopeless	I'm Ok You're NOT OK *One-up position* Attitude: Get rid of State: Angry/Defensive
	You're Not Ok with me	

This is a useful bit of psychology to apply to our relationships – we need to keep them in the empowered and healthy green box (that is actually grey in diagram – use your imagination here, please). And this is how we do that – we provide the parental guidance and support, nurturing and structure, and the expressive emotions of co-creating and playfulness. This way we keep positive emotions running through our working lives and our team's experience – we provide the care and compassion to support and help them, we keep life fun and light so that our followers can feel free to express themselves and contribute, we balance maintaining rules and processes with self-expression and emotional freedom. So what about when they go a bit wrong?

You may know what I mean, there you are thinking you're being all supportive, and someone gets the hump. Why? Or maybe you were thinking that bit of fun just went a bit too far. How?

■ *46 After Anita Mountain and Chris Davidson 2011*

It is so easy to fall out of the boxes! One minute I think I'm being all helpful and structuring and then I realise I'm actually criticising. Maybe I think I'm really helping and supporting, but actually I'm just jolly well interfering. And if I don't keep consistent in my behaviours I'm just going to mess everyone up – they just won't know where they stand.[173]

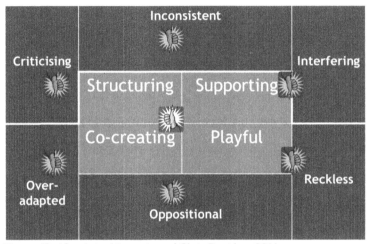

Figure 47 After Anita Mountain and Chris Davidson 2011

It's great to be playful, but not when it's reckless or uncaring. And playing devil's advocate is only good so far, then it just becomes opposing for the sake of it. And being polite and getting along with people is all very well, but being over-adapted leads to inauthenticity and manipulation – if we feel

---

[173] Mountain, A. and Davidson, C. (2011). *Working together*. Farnham, Surrey: Ashgate Pub.

we can't ask for what we need we do something manipulative instead.

There is much more on these different types of behaviours in my book Changing Vampires into Angels.[174]

So the key is to be mindful in your communication – be aware of what you are doing and model the way you want others to communicate in the team.

And beyond all else, keep in your mind the most important thing of all, that when we accept people completely for who they are, no matter what they do, we can correct the behaviours and attitudes we don't like and that don't work for us, while all the time keeping them fully emotionally engaged.

---

[174] Paviour, M (2002) *Changing Vampires into Angels - 6 Steps to Heaven in your relationships* Isiliver Books ISBN 0954365402

CHAPTER 14
The Love Human

I don't think that it is co-incidental that I'm basing my leadership model on work done by Dr Helen Fisher on love! Isn't that wonderful? From love and understanding why we fall in love we have discovered how we can be better leaders. And she has some fantastic research on women in leadership saying that "tomorrow belongs to women," and that women and their natural talents are changing the world, making them ideal leaders and successful shapers of business and society--today and on into the twenty-first century.[175]

---

175 Fisher, H. (1999). *The first sex*. New York: Ballantine Books.

I've always found Helen Fisher's work fascinating, but, naturally, my interest was initially recreational. I'm just one of those people who love psychology so much I can't help but read just about as much as I can, in all sorts of areas, because, in the end, we are just humans and we don't draw a line between being a work human, a home human and a love human.

On the other hand, I like the idea that we are really all love humans all the time.

Helen Fisher talks about 4 Brain systems, and she has linked this to four personality types suggesting that some people have a higher density of certain Neurotransmitter or brain chemicals or are more likely to invoke that system.

This is the neuroscience of trait behaviour. It's new and (the wonderful) Helen Fisher is still experimenting to see if the 64 genes they have identified can be directly linked to personality trait and behaviour.[176] Dr Helen has very kindly allowed me to use her questionnaire based upon the Fisher Temperament Inventory to help me to identify leadership qualities. This means that we can apply Dr Helen's amazing research to

---

[176]Brown, L., Acevedo, B. and Fisher, H. (2013). Neural Correlates of Four Broad Temperament Dimensions: Testing Predictions for a Novel Construct of Personality. *PLoS ONE*, 8(11), p.e78734.

working life, and with some cross referencing to other psychologists and their research we have been able to put together this brand new view of leadership!

Dr Helen is looking at the neuroscience of temperament and personality by innovatively combining the science with anthropology.

I love the way that neuroscience is catching up with psychology. Psychologists and philosophers have talked about traits and personality since time immemorial and now we are linking these ideas to actual brain systems. Wow!

Changing your body chemistry

In the next bit we are going to invoke each of the brain systems, so this is a practical part of the book, I want you to try to carry out the exercises, and then reflect on how you are feeling. Now, remembering that you may not be very granular, I'm not asking you to write an essay (not that is unless you are very granular and you feel the need to do so) it's a matter of awakening your awareness. As an A+B leader you need to develop your self-awareness.

In Emotional Intelligence terms this is about noticing behaviours and responses. In Affective terms I am happy with you just noticing how and why you feel and where you feel it.

I commence each of the four sections on different brain systems with an "invoking activity" which is intended to help you to get a taste for how that system feels when you are "in it". It's also intended to be fun, by the way, so enjoy.

I then ask you to reflect on the activity and ask you questions that will help you to identify aspects of that particular brain system on you.

Following on from this I describe how the brain system can make you feel, and the icon we use which is intended to act as illustration and reminded about the brain system in question.

Next, using Helen Fishers profile types, I describe a person who favours this brain system, what type of leader they would make, how they interact with their followers and how they behave when under pressure.

Finally, I draw comparisons with the brain system and other trait models including Belbin's Team Traits and Kolb's Learning Styles.

The aim is to provide an opportunity for the reader to do a bit of self-assessment and see if you can identify helpful factors in increasing your self-awareness, and also in looking at how to better deal with things that you may find specifically challenging, even if some others do not.

What are your brain system preferences?

Helen Fisher has identified four personality trait types based on the 4 brain systems. These personality types don't hibernate when it's time to go to work, so we can use the same traits to look at how you use these to lead, and how using different styles can be related to different brain systems. This means that you can facilitate a style of leadership by invoking the right body chemistry.[177]

Warning!

I want to make it abundantly clear that leadership is not a matter of getting a dopamine fix (or whatever) and then launching into a situation. What I am suggesting is that the brain system will help to create the right mind set for you, and also that you probably prefer one or two over the others. In understanding your preferences and in knowing how to create the right body chemistry for tackling different situations you will be helping yourself to be more successful.

Believe me, if there was a Leadership pill I would tell you (although I rather think natural remedies are best when talking about emotions!)

---

[177] Fisher Temperament Inventory –Fisher, H

CHAPTER 15
The Serotonin leadership brain

Dr Helen Fisher described people with this brain system preference as "builders" a term she now wishes she had not used! Here, I describe this preference as a coach/builder. I understand why Helen may have misgivings: when talking about personality people don't want to seem dull – why would they; and the serotonin brain system type is certainly not dull!

These people may be able to keep a balance in their lives, but they certainly know the value of truth and honesty and integrity – to such as extent that they will often stand up for what is right, no matter what.

Being serotonin-brained doesn't mean being torpid or inactive. Some of my favourite leaders, my most inspiring leaders have been serotonin. They are good listeners, and able coaches.

Serotonin is noted in the ventrolateral prefrontal cortex, which is where we make decisions about the emotional and behavioural significance of situations – in other words our values.

Now, invoke some serotonin and find out more.

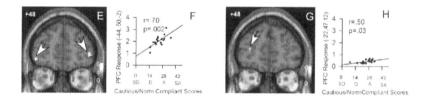

48 Coach Leader (serotonin brain) area activated: ventrolateral prefrontal cortex. Source: Neural Correlates of Four Temperament Dimensions. Brown, Acevedo and Fisher 2013

Invoking Activity

Get up and take a walk around the room, and at every opportunity fist bump a friend or colleague or family member, and while you do so, tell them about a happy memory that you have. It must be happy. Then repeat the exercise with a handshake, and then do the same with another person but with a two handed handshake.

Keep walking round, looking for people to whom you can tell your happy memory.

Finally, get someone to give you a shoulder massage while you tell them the happy memory, and return the favour. Ideally, you could get a small group of people to stand in a circle and give each other a shoulder massage for a few moments.

Reflection

Now notice what you feel right now.

- How alert do you feel?
- How relaxed/tense do you feel?
- What are you thinking; upbeat thoughts or pessimistic thoughts?
- How do you feel about yourself?
- How easy would it be to resist a temptation right now, if you had to?
- How do you feel about someone who recently annoyed you, in this very minute – or do you resist thinking about that person, or anything else that annoyed recently?

How serotonin can make you feel

When your serotonin is at a good level you feel mellow and relaxed, hopeful and optimistic. You feel at peace with the world and everyone in it...ahhh! In this state you feel creative, thoughtful, and focused. You also have a lot of impulse control, which enables you to "just say no" more easily when someone walks in with the biscuit tin. Basically, you are totally chilled, but still alert, not drowsy and ready for sleep, just ...feeling good.

It will be no surprise that Serotonin is known as a happiness brain chemical. And it's a certain hmmmm kind of happiness. Lovely.

The Serotonin system icon

49 Coach -Builder Brain System Icon

Serotonin is produced when we sit in the sun. It gives us that lovely relaxed and at peace feeling. For this reason we have designated the symbol for serotonin as a little sunshine, because when you get a hit of serotonin it's like the sun is shining in your heart (well brain actually, but you know what I mean).

Our serotonin woman is shown being active, because gentle exercise is also a good way of promoting serotonin.

Interestingly, when you experience happy memories this also gives your serotonin levels a boost.

High Serotonin Brain Activity – The Coach

High levels of Serotonin are associated with sociability and feelings of calm. And so The Coach tends to be very calm, persistent and co-operative. The Coach has a managerial style, they are very protective of others and behave with extraordinary loyalty and consistency. As a result they are usually very popular bosses who engender a strong team spirit. The Coach will appreciate the importance of work life balance and will want to support their team members in this regard.

Dr. Fisher describes this type as Builders and says "The Builders live in the suburbs and in the countryside. They want grass and neighbourhoods and to be part of the PTA". The top word used by Builders in their Chemistry.com profiles is family. (178,000 profiles sample)

Dr Fisher's favourite example of The Coach (Builder) is President George Washington, a Builder "par excellence" as Dr Fisher says in her book.

The Builder-Coach Leader[178]

The Coach Leader is calm, has very good people skills and will have an open door management policy. They will always say "good morning" to you and probably inquire about the health of your family, they will remember things about your personal life and take an interest in it. The Coach will love meetings where they can combine getting to know and socialize with people with their work. The Coach is unlikely to feel any apprehension about meeting new people.

The Coach may suggest a drink after work, or have work colleagues round to their house for supper. The Coach is likely to remain in the same organisation for a long time, as they are very loyal, so the Coach Leader may have worked his or herself up through the ranks. The Coach is likely to have long term friends from work and will keep in touch with people who leave. They may even find that this is useful as they can use their network to find the right people or suppliers for different roles or requirements. They will remember details about the social and personal lives of these people and this will help them find the right fit for a job.

---

[178] Fisher, H., Island, H., Rich, J., Marchalik, D. and Brown, L. (2015). Four broad temperament dimensions: description, convergent validation correlations, and comparison with the Big Five. *Frontiers in Psychology*, 6.

The Coach will follow the rules and take their responsibilities very seriously. Even if this means staying after hours to finish work, or popping round to a team members house to make sure they are ok.

The Coach will ask the difficult questions in the board room, but they are not negative. They like to be safe and secure, therefore things are always in perfect order around them and they plan well ahead.

The Coach may be the one you will hear saying "we don't do things like that around here". They are likely to suffer cognitive dissonance if things change too rapidly around them. They work in a methodical manner and are very dependable and hard-working; they are likely to get bored quickly and are very good at focusing on tasks and projects until the end.

The Coach's relationship with their team

The Coach will stand by their team members and support them, even in the face of overwhelming evidence to the contrary, because they prize loyalty and deliver on this.

The Coach will be a very solid and straight forward leader, they will be cautious and not get carried away with new ideas, they will want to have a proper business case before deviating, and it will have to be thoroughly investigated and proven before they opt to change from their usual pathway.

The Coach may well have people from other departments seeking them out for support as they are so strong and dependable members of the organization and they like to consider themselves a part of the organization's community. Other people tend to turn to them in times of need.

CASE STUDY: THE SEROTONIN LEADER

Petrina Mayson – CEO The Now! Group of Charities

When Petrina (Trina) Mayson became CEO of the Now! charity group Ltd she knew she had found the perfect job; perfect because through it she can live her very real and very practical values. Yes, this is a serotonin leader, so please do expect me to say the word values rather too often (as they are usually not spoken about often enough).

Some people get involved in wrong doing, some collaborate with wrong doers, and some become bystanders. And then there are the resisters, who just say "no". Trina is just such a "resister", and she has proven that ethics and leadership actually do go together rather well.

Having experienced the worst of workplace bullying and unethical, indeed fraudulent, behaviour in her early years in management, Trina says she had no choice but to act, and even though she had little support, she went ahead, anyway. The stress of taking such huge responsibility did affect her health – and this is something she is mindful about now.

For her the greatest piece of learning in all of this was overcoming her disbelief that people could behave so unethically – she says this was her naivety – but perhaps it is just that her values are so unassailable that to be other than true to ones ideals is simply unthinkable. So, Trina learnt that not everyone lives by ethical values – but it has done nothing to deter her from living to hers – no matter what. If the values don't fit – she simply cannot do the job.

Trina says she doesn't like rules, but actually, she does love structure, she just can't abide rules that reinforce or support behaviour that she simply sees as wrong. Ah, there are those values again – running through her like a stick of Eastbourne rock!

When Trina became CEO of Now! Charity Group Ltd her plan was to first understand it in absolute detail – to know what everyone did, to know all the clients – and then to decide how to fulfil its mission. One of the first (unpopular) decisions was to close down the only training offered by the charity – at that time – a "free of charge" art class used by relatively well-off people in a well-heeled local town. Yes, they had participants, but Trina could not support it when the people on the course could probably afford to join evening classes.

So, out with the old and in with the new - Trina re-invented training.

First of all, if the charity was going to successfully attract people who really needed it, it had to be a softly, softly approach. "Why tell people that they are going to be assessed for qualifications?" asks Trina , "It only makes them stressed" and many of the people the "Now Charity" deal with would be likely to run a mile – so they have created a system that assesses the client as they work so that they don't know that assessment is happening – until they are presented with their qualification certificate!

Trina has thrown away the rule book on how to assess training, yes, but she had brought in the new "Now" rule book – one that responds to her clients' needs and to what will support their success.

The charity is setting the standard for personalised learning in the true sense – in taking people from being lonely, agoraphobic, unemployed and unemployable, to confident members of the community. She's applying this to a new project and is now also supporting the long term sick.

The "Now Charity" group run a whole raft of fabulous courses, from carpentry to Mental Health First Aider (a course they developed and subsequently run for other charities). They run apprenticeships – only not according to the rules, but by their rules – they take people who may not otherwise have got an apprenticeship – and they prove that it is the criteria for apprenticeships is the problem, not the clients; and they achieve this by demonstrating tremendous success with their apprentices.

This is what happens when a serotonin leader – driven by values and structure – gets her teeth into providing a real and needed solution for disadvantaged people; for those in poverty and for those who lack skills or education.

As a leader, Trina actually finds it hard to turn off the "find a solution" programme in her brain! She has a low key style, with her door always open and her office shared with her team, there is no sense of hierarchy, and yet there is a very real sense of whom the team are following.

Trina's approach is to build one brick at a time – gentle, slow steps until people start to run and leap on their own; with her team as well as with their clients. How fitting that a Coach Builder should find her bliss in coaching people into building new lives for themselves; one small, confident step at a time.

The Now! Charity Group Ltd recycles furniture and provides training and support for disadvantaged people and those in poverty and distress across East Sussex: www.furniturenow.org.uk

The Coach under pressure

The Coach can, however, be rather pedantic in the approach, they can become "Mentor Vampires", absolutely stuck on their one "right way of doing things" and consequently they can become hostile towards other solutions and rather than coaching, they can become overly advisory, so that you feel you are being cornered into one way of doing things.

The Coach can even be pig-headed sometimes as they will tenaciously keep hold of their plans, no matter what organizational changes may be taking place.

They value security so highly that sometimes these affable leaders can, when under pressure, start quoting the law, the union rules and ancient policies in order to maintain their position and prevent change. They can become pessimistic and far too rigid, taking things literally – sometimes taking offence.

The Coach Team Type

Belbin's team traits[179] may place them as a Co-ordinator, Implementer Resource Investigator and/or Team Worker as they love to be sociable and are great in situations where they need to network or bring different people together around the table.

Co-ordinators are task orientated individuals who like to consider feasible and practical solutions, rather than creative or imaginative ones. Clarifies goals and promotes decision making.

Resource investigators seek to support the team's effort by being on the look out for different resources and ideas from outside the team. They develop contacts, are extravert and enthusiastic

---

[179] Belbin, Team Roles

Implementers are the pragmatists and are able to put general ideas and plans into action.

Team workers - The strength of this role is the ability to perceive the needs of the individuals and thus, by supporting the individuals enable the group to collaborate and maintain its cohesion.

The Coach Learning Type –Pragmatist

The Coach will learn from their mistakes, and this may make them very cautious about trying something that didn't work in the past. They like to make sure they plan thoroughly and will be happy to develop and project manage a new venture, rather than come up with the new idea themselves.

In keeping with their love of plans and details, The Coach may prefer to learn by applying ideas to real situations. An idea needs to work in reality for them to consider it.[180]

Pragmatist:

Pragmatists are keen on trying out ideas, theories and techniques to see if they work in practice. They positively

---

[180] Alice Kolb , David A. Kolb Encyclopedia of the Sciences of Learning pp 1698-1703
Kolb's Learning Styles

search out new ideas and take the first opportunity to experiment with applications. They are the sorts of people who return from management courses brimming with new ideas that they want to try out in practice. They like to get on with things and act quickly and confidently on ideas that attract them. They tend to be impatient with ruminating and open-ended discussions. They are essentially practical, down to earth pile who like making practical decisions and solving problems. They respond to problems and opportunities "as a challenge". Their philosophy is: "There is always a better way" and "if it works it's good".

CHAPTER 16
The Dopamine Leadership Brain

The Dopamine, or Explorer (as Helen Fisher calls them), brain system is often the one we associate with leadership. These perceived to be the high-fiving, achievers who have boundless energy and drive.

Actually, Explorers may not be like that at all! Many will love bungee jumping and mountain climbing, but they may just as well like reading, or puzzling. The Explorer may explore the inner as well as the outer life.

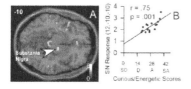 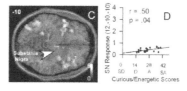

50: Explorer Leader (dopamine brain) area activated: substantia nigra region. Source: Neural Correlates of Four Temperament Dimensions. Brown, Acevedo and Fisher 2013

Invoking Activity

Can you skip? Some people (mainly men, apparently) find this difficult, and if you are one of them, then try an alternative exercise (such as reaching up vertically whilst jumping from foot to foot and then doing the same horizontally) . If you find it easy to skip, then that is what I'm going to ask you to do. Skip around the room, down the corridor, out onto the street, I don't care where you skip, just skip for all you are worth! Keep going with this for about 3 minutes or more.

Reflection

Now notice what you feel right now.

- How alert do you feel?
- How relaxed/tense do you feel?
- What were you thinking?
- How do you feel about yourself?

- What facial expression did you have while you were skipping – do you still have expression on your face? And if so, to what extent?
- Did you laugh?

How dopamine can make you feel

Don't be fooled into thinking that dopamine is some kind of drug that our brain is clever enough to make for us so we can all feel the wonderful effects. Dopamine is a Neurotransmitter and it has many different functions, crossing various synapses to create many different pathways. However, we are particularly looking at how it relates to the emotions and what drives us.

Dopamine causes that "yes!" feeling. In psychological terms, that moment of success when we win and we raise our arms into the air in victory is an outcome of a rush of dopamine. This is in the mesolimbic system of the brain, because this is the bit that relates to pleasure and reward, and this is the bit that concerns us here. However, it's worth noting that dopamine isn't there to make you feel good, it's there to send a signal, and sometimes that signal, which is a "do it again" signal, can be responsible for us repeating behaviours that were not so very good; such as losing on a horse in a race. We may get the same type of feel good from the loss as we do from the win. It's that "near miss" feeling that can provoke us to act in ways that are, essentially, risky.

Because dopamine, which floods into your system when you're positive, has two functions, not only can it make you happier in a kind of energised way, it turns on all of the learning centres in your brain allowing you to adapt to the world in a different way.

The Dopamine system icon

Our dopamine woman is holding her hands in the air in the position known as "Fierro" so named by psychologist Isabella Poggi. This means pride, but because in English pride can have some negative connotations, we use the Italian word which means proud of oneself without being arrogant. It's a very positive sense of pride.

51 Explorer Brain System Icon

Fierro is a universal human gesture, no matter where you go in the world, people use this gesture to indicate success and pride. It's not just Usain Bolt or Mo Farrah, even congenitally blind people will use this pose when they succeed – which was seen in the Olympics. In other words, we do not learn this from seeing people doing it, we innately use this gesture.

As dopamine's job, among others is to boost our pleasure centre we have used little stars to indicate dopamine, as these demonstrate both the "stars" of achievement and also the twinkling feel good upbeat and driven or energised feeling we can get when this pathway is enabled.

High Dopamine Brain Activity – The Explorers[181]

High levels of Dopamine are associated with curiosity and spontaneity. And so Explorers tend to be very adventurous and curious. They often love activities that they can get all physical about.

Explorers are also very creative – they love to allow their thinking to run wild and try out novel ideas. However, this trying out of novel ideas may make them a tad impulsive. The Explorer may want to go for broke while some of the less adventurous types are saying "you know you should do a risk assessment first."

---

[181] Curious/Energetic: Fisher, H., Island, H., Rich, J., Marchalik, D. and Brown, L. (2015). Four broad temperament dimensions: description, convergent validation correlations, and comparison with the Big Five. *Frontiers in Psychology*, 6.

The thing is, they can also be difficult to convince. Once they have an idea in their head they are not likely to be easily swayed. I've recently watched that marvellous TV series "Mr. Selfridge" about that ubiquitous Explorer based on the book "Shopping, Seduction and Mr. Selfridge" by Lindy Woodhead. He was a perfect example of that risk taking, driven and energizing leader, who inspired with his charm and his belief in new ways. And of course, his gambling and pleasure seeking were also a feature of his Explorer ways. In fact, his story tells us that Explorers can make the most amazing leaders, but they also need to curb their risk taking if they are going to have long term success.

Generally speaking men are more likely to be Explorers than women, not by a large percentage, but the sample number Fisher used was sufficiently large to make the one percentage point difference relevant.

"The Explorers want the stimulation and the novelty of the big city," says Dr. Helen Fisher, who suspects President Barack Obama is an Explorer. "He's got charm, and the Explorer has charm to kill. The high-dopamine type is comfortable in his own skin. Look at the way Obama moves. It's beautiful."

Fisher identifies a number of people she believes epitomizes the Explore type including President John F. Kennedy, Boris Yeltsin, Helen Keller (if you don't know much about her, do find out who she was). Keller had severe sensory disability, being deaf-blind and yet she went on to become a silent film star among other things!), Ernest Hemmingway, Alfred Tennyson and Robert Schumann. It is not surprising to find many creative people among the Explorers.

The top word used by Explorers in their Chemistry.com profiles is *adventure*. (178,000 profiles sample)

Explorer Leader

The Explorer Leader may be an energetic and restless person. They will not want to sit around in long drawn out meetings; they will want decisions made quickly so that action can take place straight away. They may lose interest in their scheme before its finished and be onto the next one if there are no others to keep the ball rolling and complete what they started.

Explorers may favour a Present hedonistic/ Future orientated time perspective[182]. Explorers prefer a job that gives them plenty of variety and the opportunity to solve

---

[182] Zimbardo, P and Boyd J (2010) *The Time Paradox: Using the New Psychology of Time to Your Advantage* Rider ISBN 1846041554

problems in innovative and creative ways. They love to try out a new theory and will surprise people with brand new thinking or ways of acting, often that challenge their colleagues, and the Explore may not understand why others are not as excited as they are about these new ideas.

A problem that may cause stress for another type, may well create a sense of excitement in the Explorer.

The Explorer leader may find themselves drawn to other explorers when recruiting; they will be excited and curious about people who have had an adventurous past, and may find themselves taking on people who are not ideal for the team. There are only so many creative starters that a team needs and it's vital to have some completers too. Explorers need to recognize the value that is brought to the business by those other types, they need to learn how to listen to people who express risks and not see them as "negative" or "pessimistic" but rather as beneficial barometers of reality.

If an Explorer does not feel appreciated at work, they make take extraordinary measures. Helen Fisher suggests that they are more likely to break the rules or even the law than some of the other types, but of course this is entirely dependent upon their values and how these drive them.

CASE STUDY: EXPLORER LEADER 1

Maria Paviour

When I was working in a Yoghurt factory in the 1980's in the interim between college and university, I found myself being crushed by the alienating work that I was carrying out. It involved taking yoghurt pots off a machine as they were being pushed out, and putting them onto a tray, which when filled with twelve pots was then placed, by me, onto a conveyor belt to be covered in plastic packaging for shipment to supermarkets.

I'm glad to say this type of work is no longer required and even when I was working there they were installing new computerized machinery that was going to take the place of this very labour intensive system. The down side of this was that many of the wonderful women who worked in the factory would have lost their jobs – these were women who found the hours fitted in with childcare as they started at 8am were finished by 4pm and were paid well as it was not work that many people wanted.

The effect on this Explorer was pretty devastating. At regular intervals my partner (another temporary college leaver also called Maria!) and I would look at each other and agree, silently, to knock over a yoghurt pot, causing the whole works to gum up, and consequently give me and my pal Maria to have a few moments to breathe while the machine minder sorted it all out. I felt pretty bad about this, but we both felt it was beyond our control to be able to withstand the agonizing monotony. It also brought home the reality of "alienation" at work – which I had studied in theory – but here I was living it!

CASE STUDY: EXPLORER LEADER 2

Leatham Green, Assistant Director HR
at East Sussex County Council

Leatham is another great example of an Explorer Leader. He doesn't see his thinking is any different from anyone else's – he sees his role being to "lift the lid" and for people to say "I didn't think that I had that in me" and he endeavours to inspire that by modelling it. He says he sometimes gets frustrated that the people he's leading don't see their potential, but he also sagely recognises that this is also about "life choices" – just because you could be a brain surgeon doesn't mean that you want to.

People often like to recruit people who work for Leatham, and he sees this as a huge positive, unusual, in the arena of local government, where the culture often supports the view that managers should be "about keeping people and having the view that everything will be fine if things just float in the right direction". Leatham points out, if you don't develop people and allow them to grow their skills and talent, then mediocracy will set in.

Leatham admits that he may not always feel comfortable with imposed change, but that he has to have variety. He says "If I don't have change I have to generate it through variety and innovation." He's happy with risk – seeing things that don't work as learning and asking – how can I do that better, rather than as a failure. Having said that, Leatham isn't complacent, he says "If I bake a cake and my sponge sinks, then that's a failure and I'd probably throw it in the bin – and when I was running the school meals service that could be quite important."

However, in this world of managing people and HR he may try something very innovative and different in terms of how he can engage with people differently or better, and if something doesn't land well, because perhaps no one is turning up or feedback is poor – he doesn't see that as a failure – it just tells him what won't work so he can set his mind to what would. People have fed back to Leatham that this approach does set him apart, as so many people are not prepared to try. That is a bit different, as many people aren't prepared to try in order to simply find out that it doesn't work!

Leatham believes what is important is how you frame in your mind. He says "if I generate lots of ideas not all of them will work – I may need to test 10 to get 1." This can, he admits, be challenging for the team. However, his current team have been with him for 5 years!

For example, Leatham and his team have completely torn up the rule book on how to deal with work place conflict and now, through working in collaboration with and engaging the Trade Unions, their preferred approach is mediation – and for an organisation with 16,000 to achieve this major change, to pilot test and implement within 18 months is very fast. And pace is important to him. Having said that he shows great resilience in pursuing projects until they are embedded, including appreciative enquiry (which he first introduced in 1998 and which has now become a part of standard practice) and Mindfulness, as he has been a practicing meditator since he was eighteen years old – and believes this was responsible for building his confidence and resilience – and he introduced Mindfulness in the first instance in 1991.

He admits he has been tenacious, and he sees this as related to passion – for him this passion is to be an able and inspiring (not necessarily theatrical) leader or manager, and that 16,000 people really do need a compelling reason for following where you go – and this can sometimes be with financial cuts – and we are dealing with vulnerable adults and children. We therefore must create something meaningful – a knockback does not mean you should stop. Leatham demonstrates all the qualities of learned optimism!

In the 1970's Leatham had to consider how to live his life at a time when trying to come to terms with his sexuality was tough with much intolerance– and then the first job he took in a hotel the manager told him that he needed to go on a course – it was meditation! They meditated morning and night for 10 minutes – and this was a "life saver" and helped him to recognise what really is important - and what is not!

"Life is all about compromise – but the essence of me, and what makes me tick is the same, and won't change no matter what happens - this exhilarates confidence in my team because if we give something a shot, my team know that providing they've done the groundwork (which is always essential), it'll usually work." And if not, it'll be a learning experience for everyone.

> Leatham is prepared to give his team autonomy – but expects them to come up with the solutions, he inspires them to try new things, but not to emulate him, he expects them to do it "in their *own* way".

The Explorer's relationship with their team

As bosses, Explorers can be great fun. They are likeable, tend to be happy and fun, and enjoy the people around them they make team work enjoyable. They love to play and work can almost seem like play when they are on good form. Meetings are lively and full of humour.

The Explorer under pressure

An Explorer can sometimes be unreliable – they really don't operate well without excellent PAs or assistants who can keep day to day life on the straight and narrow, and if they are good at appreciating how vital their PA is, the work can be quite rewarding. On the other hand they can find it hard to control their unpredictability. If an Explorer leader is not fully focused on the goal they can go off at a million tangents. They don't like routine and can get bored easily.

Explorers can also be impatient with team members who are not optimistic, or who try to put the brakes on a project if it has not been properly tested out, or if people are nervous of change, or do not appreciate their spontaneity and sudden changes in direction.

Explorers love change, most especially if it is their idea in the first place!

Explorer Team Type

Belbin's team traits may place them as a Resource Investigator and Plant.

Resource investigator:

This person in this role seeks to support the team's effort by being on the lookout for different resources and ideas from outside the team. Develops contacts, is extravert and enthusiastic.

Plant:

The Plant/Innovator is the creative thinker, constantly looking for, and coming up with new ideas. The innovator tends not to be very sensitive to the needs of the individual.[183]

Explorers and Learning Types - Activists

There may be a connection here between the Explorers and Kolb's learning type "Activists". Explorers are high energy,

---

[183] Belbin, Team Roles

they like feeling their bodies moving around. I'm a bit of an Explorer and one feature of my leadership style is the fact that I'd love to run up and down the stairs rather than pick up the phone to speak to my team members. I loved the feelings of movement and urgency I got from physically shifting my body from one place to another. Yes, you could say I'm a typical "high energy" Explorer.

Activists involve themselves fully and without bias in new experiences. They enjoy the here and now and are happy to be dominated by immediate experiences. They are open-minded, not sceptical, and this tends to make them enthusiastic about anything new. Their philosophy is: "I'll try anything once". They tend to act first and consider the consequences afterwards. Their days are filled with activity. They tackle problems by brainstorming. As soon as the excitement from one activity has died down they are busy looking for the next. They tend to thrive on the challenge of new experiences but are bored with implementation and longer-term consolidation. They are gregarious people constantly involving themselves with others but in doing so; they seek to centre all activities on themselves.

CHAPTER 17
The Testosterone Leadership Brain

The first thing to realise is that this has nothing to do with being male or masculine. This relates to the chemical in the "Thinky" part of the brain – the Dorsolateral Prefrontal Cortex – where we figure out how to achieve our goals. You can be elegant and very feminine and have a testosterone brain preference. So please push out of your mind any thoughts to do with gender or sex stereotypes – they not relevant nor are they welcome here!

Testosterone brainers are analytic and goal focussed. They can work things out quickly – and often visually. This temperament type can be a powerful and strong leader – assertive and clear thinking. Find out more, by invoking that high testosterone feeling.

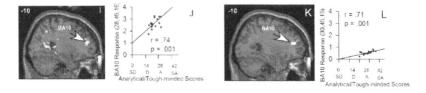

52: Director (Testosterone Brain) area activated: dorsolateral prefrontal cortex. Source: Neural Correlates of Four Temperament Dimensions. Brown, Acevedo and Fisher 2013

Invoking Activity

Spend three minutes standing with your hands on your hips, your feet a reasonable space apart and your chin up. Ideally, a slight smile upon your face .You need to feel your body as extended, and not curled up. This pose has been dubbed the "Wonder Women "pose, which may explain precisely what your need to do.

After three minutes, sit down and make notes, but ensure that you are upright, and not bent over, and that you are taking up as much space as you can with your body while you reflect.

Reflection

Now notice what you feel right now.

- How alert do you feel?
- How relaxed or tense?
- What do your stress levels feel like?
- How energised are you?

- How focussed are you?

- What do you feel like doing right now? Sorting a few things out, like tidying up cupboards or relationships, or do you feel confrontational and ready for good old row?

How Testosterone can make you feel

First of all, we all have testosterone. I know we tend to think it's a male hormone, but women have it too. What we know about testosterone is that it makes us feel powerful without necessarily feeling aggressive. Testosterone is the hormone of confidence.

Interestingly, Silver back Gorillas, the heads of the Gorilla family groups, have very high levels of testosterone. But they also have low levels of stress hormones. So they have a sense of power and authority without being reactive.

You can expect to feel the same after doing the power pose. Your levels of cortisol will have dropped. Cortisol is a stress hormone, and research from Amy Cuddy et al has demonstrated that 3 minutes in the 'wonder woman' Power Pose (see overleaf), or any of the other power poses will dramatically alter your body chemistry. Your cortisol levels will drop, and your testosterone levels will rise. Any behaviour that involves making your body larger, spreading your arms and taking up more space is likely to have the same effect.

When you review how you feel you are likely to feel positive, strong but not reactive or angry.

53Maria Paviour, Power Posing

The Testosterone system icon

Our high testosterone woman is standing in a power pose. When the system is working at its best for leaders it is this power, authority without reactivity or aggression that demonstrates this brain system at its best.

54 Director Brain System Icon

For the same reason the symbol for testosterone activity is an oak tree. Standing firm, tall and unyielding, it is strong and powerful yet silent.

High Testosterone Activity - Directors

Although testosterone is thought of as a male hormone, it does occur in both sexes, but without doubt is dominant in men. There are fewer women who display this characteristic 9.7% of women as opposed to 24.8% of men. Directors are analytical, decisive, focused, inventive, competitive, independent and strategic-minded. They are also daring, original, direct, non-conforming, and skilled at abstract thinking and short-term planning, often assertive, tough-minded and efficient.

Directors can be competitive and driven, and frequently are considered aggressive. The Director has to win, be the best and they often do achieve these things, rising to the top of organizations and gaining positions of authority and power. The top word used by Directors in their Chemistry.com profiles is intelligence. (178,000 profiles sample).

Examples of famous Directors provided by Helen Fisher include Albert Einstein, Bill Gates, Hillary Clinton (whose partner Bill is a Negotiator) and Dr Phil McGraw.

Directors as leaders

Bold and uncompromising, Directors are pragmatic, hard-nosed decisive individuals. They enjoy challenges and are rarely fazed by them; they almost enjoy the thrill of a problem that they can solve. Directors certainly "keep their heads when all about them, are losing theirs" to quote Rudyard Kipling. And even in the face of tough decisions, they usually manage to make a decision, even when faced with difficult choices.

Directors have a single-minded and focused view of work, they like to have difficult goals and they pursue them relentlessly. They solve problems by rational analysis, logical reasoning and objectivity. This can mean that they sometimes lack creativity and playfulness. Directors do not like to be unprepared and rarely fall into traps.

They pay attention to what is going on and enjoy details. They like to know everything about everything, and often act as though they do, when they may not be that well informed. But you can be sure that a Director will find out, if she needs to know. She will like having everything in her life tied down. Directors make a bee-line towards their goals and achieve them with great speed.

Directors are often good at understanding technical things and how machines work or systems operate, they are often good at sorting out issues with computers – they will not be the one being told by the IT department that they had merely forgotten to the turn the PC on!

Director's relationship with their team

Due to their uncompromising style Directors are sometimes considered to be unemotional, cold and calculating. They are seen as career focused and more interested in their own goal than the team. In fact, Directors may take the attitude that they will trample on a lot of people to get to where they want be.

Directors are not good at social skills, their attempts at humour can be unconsciously cruel or inappropriate, they do not see any need to be more friendly, and can create disharmony in the team as they will demand the information they want, and may be a bit snidely in an attempt at light-hearted criticism.

At the same Directors may miss social nuances but they are loyal and dedicated to the organization and the team. They believe themselves to be team players but can be over confident and come across as arrogant, particularly with their pernickety adherence to punctuality and precision. They do not like to be out-smarted or out-witted.

Directors are likely to have a low emotional valence focus, and probably won't notice what is happening in the team. They are unlikely to realize that one team member has broken up with her boyfriend and another is off colour that day.

Directors are likely to react quite quickly without reflecting or consideration time. And enjoy meetings where there is plenty of competitive conversation and debate. They will be direct, and to the point, but team members can be taken aback by this and may feel that the Director doesn't listen to them or appreciate that they do have good intellect too. Directors can sometime challenge and play devil's advocate too much.

Directors will not see time taken to build a relationship as necessary and they tend to see the world in black and white terms, without shades of grey. They can make inappropriate comments from time to time, and often need another type to smooth the ruffled feathers they leave behind.

Directors under pressure

Directors will offer new ideas, and they will graft their way to a solution. If that means they have to make unpopular decisions, so be it. Dangerous ways don't stifle them at all. Their persistence is often the key to their success. Under pressure a Director may revert to a pacemaker style of leadership, and forget the importance of social skills. They can be hard-nosed and fiery, and if they don't manage their emotions well they can become aggressive.

The Director Team Type

Shaper

Like the Co-ordinator this is a leader role. This individual acts more directly, however, and tries to directly shape the thinking and consequently the decisions of the group. Challenging, dynamic, thrives on pressure

Monitor/evaluator

This person is able to analyse ideas, suggestions and issues objectively.

The Director Learning Style – Theorist

Theorists adapt and integrate observations into complex but logically sound theories. They think problems through in a vertical, step-by-step logical way. They assimilate disparate facts into coherent theories. They tend to be perfectionists who won't rest easy until things are tidy and fit into a rational scheme. They like to analyse and synthesise. They are keen on basic assumptions, principles, theories models and systems thinking. Their philosophy prizes rationality and logic. "If it's logical it's good". Questions they frequently ask are: "Does it make sense?" "How does this fit with that?" "What are the basic assumptions?" They tend to be detached, analytical and dedicated to rational objectivity rather than anything subjective or ambiguous. Their approach to problems is consistently logical. This is their "mental set" and they rigidly reject anything that doesn't fit with it. They prefer to maximise certainty and feel uncomfortable with subjective judgments, lateral thinking and anything flippant.

Directors employ theoretical ways of thinking and they like to learn from understanding and applying theories.

The NHS "Values Rift"

Lorissa Page, Assistant Director of HR at Brighton and Sussex University Hospitals Trust has experience of how a lack of engagement in the NHS is causing a values rift. Like many NHS managers and clinicians, Lorissa's strongly driven by the important values of the organisation, but finds it very difficult to ratify the values that underlie the purpose of the NHS and the values that underlie the practice of people management. Lorissa's interest in employee engagement sparked off her intense interest and further studies in this area.

As a whole, Lorissa also feels that the NHS has a very bad habit of focussing on the role and needs of the nurses and doctors, and whilst they are of course an extremely important part of the NHS, the institution cannot under-value those professionals who support and maintain the system. It is the system which is not working.

This point is echoed by a dear friend of mine, Emma, who is an NHS project manager, and who has just come back from a year of volunteering in Africa. She points out how the first people to be blamed are always "NHS management". There is no doubt that Emma has values drivers – and a very keen intellect – but the NHS culture can create a rift between the values which the employees go to work to deliver upon, and the **value** that it places upon those employees.

Lorissa says that it is very clear to her that there isn't enough focus on Engagement in the NHS. Lorissa believes that the implementation of targets within the NHS are having a very negative effect on both the system's functioning as well as on the emotional engagement of the people - as these targets assume that the system is functioning and the added stress of unattainable targets is extremely detrimental on the wellbeing of the NHS' employees; Lorissa said: "The focus on Operational success overwhelms engagement."

So what would be the neurochemical way to deal with the issue of targets and performance? Ben Andrews, of KMG Health Partners has an idea. As an expert in reintegrating employees post sickness absence he suggests that the only measure needed to demonstrate performance in the NHS is the measure of patient satisfaction. Now, we've been very tardy in listening to patients, and the PROMS approach or Patient Recorded Outcome Measures is relatively new. PROMS takes patient's feedback about how they feel about a treatment and uses it as a relevant measure. Not rocket science, is it? But it's only recently that subjective feedback has been considered worth collecting!

If we take that idea and record the experience a patient perceives they have had, and the effectiveness of the treatment or consultation, we are altering the position from which we view what is or is not success in the NHS. So, if we are assuming that the amount of time you wait is a measure of poor service, we miss a whole raft of other factors. However, if we ask the individual what they felt about the service, it may be that the time they waited was not as important as the outcome.

My colleague and one time senior partner, Dr Jim Oliver would probably fail terribly on waiting times!! He's a GP, and the most popular one I've ever known. Being popular has made him a victim of his own success – he is highly sought after and patients refuse to see other GP's because they believe that the quality of care (not just treatment, but care) that they receive from him is second to none. When I've been in his surgery, I sometime hear patients saying that they've been waiting for a little while, but that they consider it worth it. The usual comment is something like, "well, you're prepared to wait for quality". Yes, I've actually heard people say this. And who wouldn't be prepared to wait a few minutes, if we get a quality of care that we believe is the best possible?

Surely, the time taken cannot be the only useful measure of patient care? Surely it is the least effective? I've managed a GP whose patient appointments were frequently around 2 minutes – this would qualify him as being the best GP in the land if we take the view that this is a measure of good patient care. On the other hand, when those 2 minute appointments include "counselling for a termination of pregnancy", then you realise that "fast" is rarely "best".

Dr Oliver works very hard to keep to time, but he does not let this hamper what he sees as the most important part of his job, listening to patients, supporting them and caring for them. As a result, I'm delighted to say that adjustments have been made by the surgery to ensure that he is able to spread appointments out more – but there is a downside. As Dr Oliver gives more time to each individual patient, he loses his between surgery times; this means he has to work late to complete all his paperwork and to call back the many people who leave a message for him. And he will call back or visit every single one.

I was very privileged to work for such a compassionate a values driven person as Jim Oliver. I'm sad to say that this was not the view of the partners in his last surgery, where he was bullied horrendously and ultimately locked out as a result of raising serious concerns of malpractice.

Jim is typical of a doctor who is transactionally engaged with the NHS; but emotionally engaged (none more so) with his patients. The NHS needs to fix this disconnect. The solution is a bottom up strategy. Listen to the patients, listen to the clinicians who are listening to the patients and use the skills of great leaders like Lorissa Page and Tracy Boylin to manage the delivery of what will support those interacting directly with the patients.

The solution is to focus on emotional engagement of employees and measuring the happiness of both the employees and the patients is the first step in this.

Why NHS targets are not just doomed to fail but creating a psychopathic culture

One of my managers, Reace McDonnell, hit the nail on the head, when he talked about how targets can create a tyrannical culture where managers who drive people hard to hit targets, may achieve the target, but damage the people in the process, undermine the values, and may even cut corners. However, when the achievement of those targets is rewarded then, by extension, it rewards the behaviour that achieved them. This, in turn, reinforces behaviours that ultimately become bullying.

NHS targets have created a culture of micromanagement and threat. And we wonder why whistle blowers are not heard.

CHAPTER 18
Oestrogen/Oxytocin Leadership Brain

This brain system seems to relate strongly to the ability to connect and empathise – Helen Fisher calls it the Negotiator, I call it the Connector/Negotiator, as these leaders seem to value human connection most highly.

Interestingly, the part of the brain activated by oxytocin is the Inferior frontal gyrus – the area noted for words and their meanings – which makes sense for the Connector! This part is also related to Broca's area which is the region for syntax and sounds. Communication is key with this brain system.

These leaders tend to be loved by their teams – because they are heard and feel understood by their leaders.

Try invoking this brain system and enjoy an oxytocin feeling.

55: Connector/Negotiator Leader (Oxytocin Brain) Area activated: inferior frontal gyrus. source: Neural Correlates of Four Temperament Dimensions. Brown, Acevedo, Fisher 2013

Invoking Activity

You will need a partner for this, by which I mean a friend or family member– or even an adored pet dog or cat (dogs are best actually, and that's not my bias talking it just is the way it is).

Take about 3 minutes to look deeply into the eyes of your partner (or dog) and either tell him or her about all the things that make you feel good, and especially anything about that person in particular that makes you feel good.

If possible, sit making some physical contact – such as holding hands, but you don't have to limit it to this. Essentially, you must make eye contact during this activity.

Reflection

Now notice what you feel right now.

- How alert do you feel?
- How relaxed or tense?
- How emotional do you feel right now?
- What do you feel like doing right now? Sorting a few things out, like tidying up cupboards or relationships, or do you feel confrontational and ready for good old row?

How Oxytocin can make your feel

Oxytocin is known as the "cuddle hormone" because it is the feeling you get when you have a really nice cuddle. Like when you come home from a rotten day at work and you are greeted with a loving hug, and all the troubles of the world appear to melt away. That feeling is oxytocin.

The Oxytocin system icon

56Connector Brain System Icon

Our oxytocin woman is portrayed with a partner showing how oxytocin state is one of the connector; our woman is holding hands and making eye contact with another human being.

The symbol for oxytocin activity is a heart, to indicate that this is the hormone that promotes bonding and human intimacy.

High Oestrogen/Oxytocin Activity – Connector/Negotiator

The Negotiator /connector has a high level of oestrogen activity. Although oestrogen is known as a female sex hormone do not think that this excludes men. Men are frequently this type. Dr Fisher found that about 35.8% of women are Negotiators and 20.4% of men, so while women beat the men in numbers there are still plenty of them out there and they are not likely to be feminine just as female Directors are not likely to be masculine.

Oestrogen is associated with intuition and creativity and negotiators are very imaginative, they are great communicators, and they work intuitively and are idealistic. They are friendly and agreeable and like to look inwards at themselves to reflect, they may be introspective

Helen fisher suggests these famous Connectors: Oprah Winfrey, Charles Darwin, Mohandas Karamchand Gandhi and Bill Clinton.

The top word used by Negotiators in their Chemistry.com profiles is *passion*. (178,000 profiles sample)

Connector/Negotiator As leaders

As a leader the Connector Negotiator will be good at seeing the big picture. They often have very high emotional valence focus and are excellent at dealing with people and social situations. They appear to see right into the hearts and minds of others and, pick up what they are thinking and feeling.

They tend to be good at reading facial expressions, gestures, postures and tone of voice. They may have a high Arousal focus and like to be aware and analytical of their own feelings, attitudes and behaviours.

They may be quite poetic in the way they describe events and people, and they like the sounds of different words, speaking and writing fluently and rapidly.

They are very compassionate, earnest, authentic and diplomatic.

Connector/Negotiator Relationship with team

The Connector is socially minded and excels at long term planning and building consensus whilst ensuring that they are flexible, caring and supportive. They are very socially aware and skilled. They will be very interested in the people in their team and will endeavour to do all they can to be supportive and caring.

The Connector will want to know why someone has done something, and will analyse in great detail. They will be a patient and friendly mentor with a good basis in theoretical understanding that they willingly share. They tend to think contextually, and so are unlikely to take a linear approach to a problem. And if there is some ambiguity they will be happy to live with it.

Connectors can find it difficult to be assertive, and may avoid confrontation; this can mean that the team take advantage of them. They can find it difficult to be clear and put the foot down or give negative feedback. And in addition, sometimes they can spend so long wondering how to deal with an issue the thing gets out of control or the matter passes and is never properly handled.

Alternatively, they may opt for covert means, and end up trying to solve the problem through secretive means behind the backs of others.

Connector/Negotiator under pressure

Under pressure The Connector may want to throw in the towel and go home and hide under the duvet. They are not keen on situations that demand a hard-nosed approach, and do not particularly enjoy confrontation of any kind. The Connector may tell you that it will all wash out in the end, and may stick their heads in the sand. If they have a difficult person to deal with they may find themselves being manipulated or bullied in a vain attempt to keep the peace.

On the other hand, the Connector may look for ways of dealing with the difficult situation or person without doing so head on – perhaps an email may be sent that drops someone else in the poop. If push comes to shove they will probably take flight.

Connector/Negotiator Team Type

Co-ordinator, team worker or plant

Co-ordinator

This is a very task orientated individual who likes to consider feasible and practical solutions, rather than creative or imaginative ones. Clarifies goals and promotes decision making.

Teamworker

The strength of this role is the ability to perceive the needs of the individuals and thus, by supporting the individuals enable the group to collaborate and maintain its cohesion.

Plant/innovator

The innovator is the creative thinker, constantly looking for, and coming up with new ideas. The innovator tends not to be very sensitive to the needs of the individual.

The Oxytocin/Oestrogen Learning Style – Reflector

They are very flexible in their ways, and are mentally adaptable. They like to weigh up the pros and cons before making a decision, and will usually take into account the context before acting. Before they take a decision they will think through many different ways of dealing with the problem or issue.

Reflector

Reflectors like to stand back to ponder experiences and observe them from many different perspectives. They collect data, both first hand and from others, and prefer to think about it thoroughly before coming to any conclusion. The thorough collection and analysis of data about experiences and events is what counts so they tend to postpone reaching definitive conclusions for as long as possible. Their philosophy is to be cautious. They are thoughtful people who like to consider all possible angles and implications before making a move. They prefer to take a back seat in meetings and discussions. They enjoy observing other people in action. They listen to others and get the drift of the discussion before making their own points. They tend to adopt a low profile and have a slightly distant, tolerant unruffled air about them. When they act it is part of a wide picture which includes the past as well as the present and others' observations as well as their own.

CASE STUDY: OXYTOCIN LEADER

Mandy Brook of Recruitment South East

Recruitment South East Ltd takes a slightly different view of the process of recruitment – it has an "affective" model – in that it recognises, and even quotes on the website that emotions are a part of the process of looking for a job and finding the right candidate for the job.

And it isn't just words.

A chance encounter gave Mandy Brook the recruitment bug – she walked into a recruitment company with no idea of what she wanted to do, but with sales experience. They handed her a yellow pages and a phone, and she never looked back. Some years later, on hearing of the demise of this company, Mandy was inspired to start a new recruitment consultancy that would work – by doing things differently.

From humble beginnings Mandy has turned Recruitment South East into a multi-million pound enterprise with a very simple philosophy: be nice to people. It hasn't been all plain sailing. Mandy had to walk away from a business venture and at that time thought she was going to buy an antique shop and lie on the beach – but that was not to be.

Mandy has a strong preference for the Oxytocin Leadership Brain System – she is a connector/negotiator. And it just goes to prove that if you work to your strength you can be a very successful leader without having to comply with outmoded stereotypical approaches to management and leadership.

Admitting that she has a high emotional valence, Mandy is tuned in to how the people in the team are feeling, and is ready, willing and able to tackle the emotions that may be impacting in that moment - as well as on an on-going basis. This comes naturally to her, but it's a masterclass in how to reach out to people through open, non-threatening body language and, importantly, tone of voice, and use non-threatening language. Mandy is also brilliant at making people feel valued, even when they don't feel able to value themselves too highly.

Her team describe Mandy as firm but fair, and relaxed but fully aware of everything that is going on. As an influential leader who is not pushy, people follow Mandy. This style of leadership facilitates very high levels of emotional engagement and loyalty, but it has to be balanced with a focused business edge too - and yes, says Mandy, they also have KPI's at RSE.

The RSE team see themselves as problem solvers rather than sales people. Mandy tells her people, don't sell, just be likeable, listen and people will remember you when they need you. Client engagement and loyalty is also high.

The RSE approach to job seekers is about, what Mandy calls, "first getting people to that happy place" through coaching. Mandy recognises that when people are looking for a new job they are not necessarily at their most positive best. For them to succeed and give the best of themselves they often need to be coached.

And the same is true for employers, who may also need to be coached to help them clarify what they want. This is an Oxytocin business model!

CONCLUSION
Good night, sweet dreams

What makes an inspiring, effective, courageous leader? I hope I've given a dash of what this requires without treading over too much old ground. By this time your prefrontal cortex may be ready for a glass of milk and a biscuit before laying your head down upon its pillow. You could try putting the book under your pillow, but I've no evidence that the knowledge does seep upwards into your mind the way Linus in Peanuts hopes it may.

So to save you the bother, I'll give you a conclusion.

The main conclusions I've drawn from this process are that we need firstly to recognise that we are emotional creatures and that this is part of our drive to survive. To cover up our feelings and emotions or to simply pretend we don't feel them is counterproductive. On the other hand, to have emotional outbursts is not productive either.

By recognising, acknowledging and accepting our emotions we can be more in control. We need to understand our emotional refractory period, and also whether we have a high emotional valance, or whether we are more the arousal focus types. By understanding ourselves we are in a tad better position to understand others.

If a leader can do one thing to improve life for his or her followers it would be to remove the threat from work. Yes, that's it - lighten up a little.

We really do need to remember that when people feel threatened they make poorer decisions, can't concentrate and become dreadful at teamwork. This is not a good state.

So get the emotional environment right, by modelling being a human in all your glory!

Make sure you give feedback the right way, inspire people with a vision to aim for and a reason for aiming.

If you really think about your preferred brain system, and the brain systems of the people around you, you may well find that all sorts of things make sense, and with no further help from me, you can power forward into fabulousness, with your fabulous people around you (and maybe they will even be leading the way for you).

So sleep well, dream of Numskull Brainy winding down as your prefrontal cortex takes a time out. Sleep well - and get enough of it if you want to thrive.[184]

Remember that Arianne Huffington advises women to "sleep to the top". Let go of being on call 24/7, enjoy your life, get better organised and remember, that one day you will look back on your life. So make sure you don't have regrets.

Palliative nurse Bronnie Ware's book "The top five regrets of the dying" should shake you into getting plenty of perspective on this matter:

1. I wish I'd had the courage to live a life true to myself, not the life others expected of me.

2. I wish I hadn't worked so hard.

3. I wish I'd had the courage to express my feelings.

4. I wish I had stayed in touch with my friends.

5. I wish that I had let myself be happier.[185]

---

[184] Huffington, A. (n.d.). *Thrive*.

So, the answer is, to get affective and brainy! Embrace you and your favourite brain system, have more fun at work, express yourself emotionally and appropriately, notice and respond to how you affect other people, remember to connect to your colleagues as friends *and* to take time out to see your friends and to be with your family.

And finally, **choose** happiness; it really is a business solution.

---

[185] Ware, B. (2012). *The top five regrets of the dying*. London: Hay House.

About the Author

Maria Paviour qualified at London University in Biology, Psychology and Education in 1985. She has been a Board Director of a media company and worked as a Business Psychologist for her own company. A head injury in 2004 then prevented her from working for two years.

On returning to work, Maria was offered a position as Business Manager for a medical practice. She significantly improved the practice in all areas and inspection results. However, she also identified malpractice and was bullied and forced out as a whistle-blower.

As a result of her experience, Maria has developed Neurochemical Leadership™ and Neurochemical Coaching™ as the antithesis to toxic work environments. She created the CARI™ tool, which makes "the invisible, visible" with regards to corporate culture – providing both diagnosis and cure. Maria trains and develops Well Being and Engagement Practitioners for The Maria Paviour Company Ltd.

Maria also works with Patients First and campaigns for safety and justice in the NHS, where she is a leading light in the NHS Task Force™.

Maria Paviour is a registered Occupational Psychologist and holds a once a week practice in NeuroChemical Coaching™ in Harley Street, London W1; she is a conference speaker and author of "Changing Vampires into Angels – Six Steps to Heaven in your Relationships" and "28 Steps to Save Your Job and Everyone Else's".

Get in touch through the website, www.mariapaviour.com, or tweet @mariapaviour

Further Reading and References

Achor, S. (2011). *The happiness advantage*. London: Virgin.

Adair, J. (2003). *Effective strategic leadership*. London: Pan.

Adair, J. and Thomas, N. (2003). *The concise Adair on leadership*. London: Thorogood.

Amthor, F. (2012). *Neuroscience for dummies*. Mississauga, Ont.: Wiley.

Babiak, P. and Hare, R. (2006). *Snakes in suits*. New York: Regan Books.

Bakan, J. (2004). *The corporation*. New York: Free Press.

Bannatyne, D. (2010). *How to be smart with your time*. London: Orion.

Bannatyne, D. (2011). *43 mistakes businesses make--and how to avoid them*. London: Headline Pub.

Barrett, L. (1998). Discrete Emotions or Dimensions? The Role of Valence Focus and Arousal Focus. *Cognition &*

Emotion, 12(4), pp.579-599.

Barrett, L. (2006). Valence is a basic building block of emotional life. *Journal of Research in Personality*, 40(1), pp.35-55.

Bee, F. and Bee, R. (1998). *Facilitation skills*. London: Institute of Personnel Management.

Belbin, R. (1993). *Team roles at work*. Oxford: Butterworth-Heinemann.

Belbin, R. (2004). *Management teams*. Amsterdam: Elsevier Butterworth-Heinemann.

Ben-Shahar, T. (2008). *Happier*. [London, Eng.]: McGraw-Hill.

Berne, E. (1968). *Games people play*. Harmondsworth: Penguin.

Blanchard, K., Zigarmi, P. and Zigarmi, D. (1987). *Leadership and the one minute manager*. [London]: Fontana.

Boyatsis, R. (1999). *Presentation to the Linkage Conference on Emotional Intelligence*.

Boyatzis, R. (1982). *The competent manager*. New York: Wiley.

Boyatzis, R. (1994). Stimulating Self-Directed Learning Through the Managerial Assessment and Development Course. *Journal of Management Education*, 18(3), pp.304-323.

Boyatzis, R., Cowen, S. and Kolb, D. (1995). *Innovation in professional education*. San Francisco: Jossey-Bass

Publishers.

Brown, B. (2008). *I thought it was just me (but it isn't)*. New York: Gotham Books.

Brown, C. Brene. *The Gifts Of Imperfection*. Center City, Minn.: Hazelden, 2010. Print.

Brown, L., Acevedo, B. and Fisher, H. (2013). Neural Correlates of Four Broad Temperament Dimensions: Testing Predictions for a Novel Construct of Personality. *PLoS ONE*, 8(11), p.e78734.

Cherniss, C. and Adler, M. (2000). *Promoting emotional intelligence in organizations*. Alexandria, VA: ASTD.

Csikszentmihalyi, M. (2002). *Flow*. London: Rider.

De Bono, E. (1968). *The 5 day course in thinking*. London: Allen Lane, the Penguin Press.

De Bono, E. (1990). *Lateral thinking for management*. London: Penguin Books.

De Bono, E. (1994). *Parallel thinking*. London: Viking.

De Pree, M. (1989). *Leadership is an art*. New York: Doubleday.

Ekman, P. (2004). *Emotions revealed*. London: Phoenix.

Emmons, R. (2007). *Thanks!*. Boston: Houghton Mifflin Co.

Fennell, M. (1999). *Overcoming low self-esteem*. London: Robinson.

Festinger, L. (1962). *A theory of cognitive dissonance*. Stanford, Calif.: Stanford University Press.

Fisher, H. (2009). *Why him? why her?*. New York: H. Holt.

Gilbert, D. (2007). *Stumbling on happiness*. London: Harper Perennial.

Ginsburg, H. and Opper, S. (1979). *Piaget's theory of intellectual development*. Englewood Cliffs, N.J.: Prentice-Hall.

Goleman, D. (1996). *Emotional intelligence*. London: Bloomsbury.

Goleman, D. (1999). *Working with emotional intelligence*. London: Bloomsbury.

Goleman, D., Boyatzis, R. and McKee, A. (2002). *The new leaders*. London: Little, Brown.

Greenfield, S. (2002). *The private life of the brain*. London: Penguin.

Hare, R. (1999). *Without conscience*. New York: Guilford Press.

Harmon-Jones, E., Harmon-Jones, C., Amodio, D. and Gable, P. (2011). Attitudes toward emotions. *Journal of Personality and Social Psychology*, 101(6), pp.1332-1350.

Harris, T. (1973). *I'm OK -- you're OK*. London: Pan Books Ltd.

Harvey-Jones, J. (1994). *All together now*. London: Heinemann.

Hill, P. (2004). *Concepts of coaching*. London: ILM.

Huffington, A. (n.d.). *Thrive*. WH Allen, Ebury Publishing.

Hunter, J., Schmidt, F. and Judiesch, M. (1990). Individual differences in output variability as a function of job complexity. *Journal of Applied Psychology*, 75(1), pp.28-42.

Kim, S. (2013). Neuroscientific Model of Motivational Process. *Frontiers in Psychology*, 4.

Lane, R., Chua, P. and Dolan, R. (1999). Common effects of emotional valence, arousal and attention on neural activation during visual processing of pictures. *Neuropsychologia*, 37(9), pp.989-997.

Lusch, R. and Serpkenci, R. (1990). Personal Differences, Job Tension, Job Outcomes, and Store Performance: A Study of Retail Store Managers. *Journal of Marketing*, 54(1), p.85.

McClelland, D. (1998). Identifying Competencies with Behavioral-Event Interviews. *Psychological Science*, 9(5), pp.331-339.

Meyer, P. (2010). *Liespotting*. New York: St. Martin's Press.

Nelson, N. (2012). *Make More Money by Making Your Employees Happy*. 1st ed. [ebook] MindLab Publishing. Available at: http://www.amazon.co.uk/Make-Money-Making-Employees-Happy-ebook/dp/B007Y9ZW12/ref=sr_1_1?s=books&ie=UTF8&qi d=1441619230&sr=1-1&keywords=Make+More+Money+by+Making+Your+Empl oyees+Happy [Accessed 7 Sep. 2015].

Northouse, P. (2004). *Leadership*. Thousand Oaks, Calif.: Sage.

O'Brien, S. (2008). *Wesley the owl*. New York: Free Press.

Orlick, T. (2008). *In pursuit of excellence*. Champaign: Human Kinetics.

Pesuric, A. and Byham, W. (1996). The New Look of Behaviour Modelling. *Training and Development*. [online] Available at: https://www.questia.com/read/1G1-18592750/the-new-look-of-behavior-modeling [Accessed 7 Sep. 2015].

Peters, T. (1992). *Liberation management*. London: Macmillan.

Pink, D. (2011). *Drive*. Edinburgh: Canongate.

Popcorn, F. (2000). *EVEolution*. New York: Hyperion.

Porras, J. and Anderson, B. (1981). Improving managerial effectiveness through modeling-based training. *Organizational Dynamics*, 9(4), pp.60-77.

Richman, L. (1994). HOW TO GET AHEAD IN AMERICA Climbing in your career calls for being clear about your personal goals, learning how to add value, and developing skills you can take anywhere. *Fortune*. [online] Available at: http://archive.fortune.com/magazines/fortune/fortune_archive /1994/05/16/79297/index.htm [Accessed 7 Sep. 2015].

Roddick, A. (1991). *Body & soul*. London: Ebury Press.

Seligman, M. (2003). *Authentic happiness*. London: Nicholas Brealey.

Seligman, M. (2006). *Learned optimism*. New York: Vintage Books.

Spencer, L. and Spencer, S. (1993). *Competence at work*.

New York: Wiley.

Spencer, L., McClelland, D. and Spencer, S. (1994). *Competency assessment methods*. [U.S.?]: Hay/McBer Research Press.

TEDxCSU 2013 Expanding Your Perspectives: The Three Myths of Behavioural Change, Cross, J, (2013). [TV programme] YouTube: TEDxCSU.

Walter V. Clarke Associates. (1996). *Activity vector analysis: Some applications to the concept of emotional intelligence.* Pittsburgh, PA: Walter V. Clarke Associates.

Williams, M. and Penman, D. (2011). *Mindfulness - the eight week meditation programme for a frantic world.* [CD] Hatchette Digital.

Zimbardo, P. (2009). *The Lucifer effect.* London: Rider.

Zimbardo, P. and Boyd, J. (2010). *The time paradox.* London: Rider.

Index

Lightning Source UK Ltd.
Milton Keynes UK
UKOW06f2018020616

275502UK00018B/429/P